*Your Tr[ue]...
able to find you
Love yourself,
Bent*

EMOTIONAL TRAUMA RELEASE TECHNIQUE™
THE ULTIMATE SYSTEM FOR RELEASING LIFE TRAUMAS

Dr. Jeffrey Benton DC CTN ACN QME

© 2022 Benton Chiropractic Media, Inc.
ISBN: 978-1-7375904-0-8
E-book ISBN: 978-1-7375904-1-5
Library of Congress Control Number: 2021914427

Emotional Trauma Release Technique is registered with the United States Patent and Trademark Office:
Serial Mark No. 86-241,723
Registry No. 4,697,448, Registered March 3, 2015
Patent Pending

All rights reserved
No part of this publication may be reproduced or transmitted in any form or by any means, electronic or mechanical, including photocopying, recording, or by any information storage and retrieval system, without permission in writing from the publisher, except in the case of brief quotations embodied in critical articles and reviews. It is illegal to copy this book, post it to a website, or distribute it by any other means without permission from the publisher or author.

Limits of Liability and Disclaimer of Warranty
The author and publisher shall not be liable for your misuse of the enclosed material. This book is strictly for informational and educational purposes only. The author and/or publisher do not guarantee that anyone following these techniques, suggestions, tips, ideas, or strategies will become successful. The author and/or publisher shall have neither liability nor responsibility to anyone with respect to any loss or damage caused, or alleged to be caused, directly or indirectly by the information contained in this book.

Medical Disclaimer
The medical or health information in this book is provided as an information resource only, and is not to be used or relied upon for any diagnostic or treatment purposes. This information is not intended to be patient education, does not create any patient-physician relationship, and should not be used as a substitute for professional diagnosis and treatment.

Publisher
10-10-10 Publishing
Markham, ON   Canada

Printed in Canada, 2022

For further information:
Benton Chiropractic Media Inc.
Jeffrey Benton, DC CTN ACN QME
www.ETRT.org

TABLE OF CONTENTS

Dedication vii
In Memoriam ix
Acknowledgements xi
Foreword xiii
Blessing xv
Preface xvii
Introduction xix
    My Personal Journey xx
    My Heart Broken Open xxi
    Pit of Despair xxii
    Angelic Help xxiv

Chapter One: Trauma 1
    The Neurobiology of Trauma 3
    The Scream 4
    Modern Medicine: A Nuanced Approach 5
    Trauma and Dissociation 7
    Unexpected or Shock Trauma 8
    Case Study: Joel 9

Chapter Two: Stress 13
    Emotional Splinters 19
    Stressors Have Memory 19
    Neurofeedback Therapy vs. ETRT 22
    Emotional Landmines: Tentacles of Emotional Triggers 24

Chapter Three: Emotions 27
    Where Emotions are Stored 29
    The Frequency of Emotions 33
    Exercise 35
    Map of Consciousness 35
    How Emotions Get Stuck and Overwhelm the Body 36
    Storage Warehouses of Unfinished Business 37
    Adverse Child Experiences 38
    Case Study: Date Rape Release 41
    Life Changing Experience 43
    Emotional Traumas have Physical Manifestations 43
    Testimonial: Family Trauma 46
    Disconnecting from the Emotions 48

Chapter Four: Physiological Proof of Emotional Trauma 51
    Broken Heart Syndrome 53
    The Brain in Heart 56
    Case Study: Shoulder Pain and Weakness 58

Chapter Five: Genetics vs. Epigenetics 61
    Emotional Trauma in the Genes 63
    Epigenetics and Suicide 64
    Single Nucleotide Polymorphisms (SNPs) 67
    Personal Case Study 68
    Neuro-Emotional Technique® (NET) 69
    Epigenetics, Telomeres, and Mindfulness 70

Chapter Six: Let it Go – It No Longer Serves You 73
    What is Fear? 75
    Case Study: Releasing the Past 78

Chapter Seven: Nurturance the Way We Need It 81
    Nurturance or the Lack Thereof 83
    Levels of Nurturance 84
    The Light of Love 87

Chapter Eight: Acknowledgment Heals 89
    Story of Anna O. 91

Chapter Nine: Preparing the Body for the ETRT™ 95
    ETRT vs. Psychology 97
    Third Eye or Yin Tang Point 99
    Hydration Reflex 99
    Self-Communication Reflex 100
    Allergy Reflex 101

Chapter Ten: The Emotional Trauma Release Technique™ 103
    Truth Heals 105
    Unwinding and Down-Regulating the Startle Reflex 107
    Performing ETRT™ Step by Step 107

Chapter Eleven: Mass Formation Psychosis and ETRT 113

Chapter Twelve:
My Mission: A Joyous and Harmonious Life 119
    Chiropractic 121
    True Health 124

Chapter Thirteen: Additional Case Studies 129
    Breaking the Negative Cycle 131
    Making Lemonade Out of Lemons 132
    Accidental Fall 132
    Sleepless Nights 133

Chapter Fourteen: Additional Testimonials 135

Epilogue 145
About the Author 149
From the Publisher 151
Endnotes 153
Index 159

This book is dedicated to all the children of the world
(I mean you and me).

May we always be empowered and maintain
a strong connection to our inner knowing and strength.
We are all part of one humanity.

May we all become Racket Free and Trauma Free!

IN MEMORIAM

My mother, Leah Fhŭrer and father, Moshe Berkowitz personify hard work, love, and dedication. My parents provided my siblings and me with a secure family home, built on a foundation of mutual respect for others, charity, and caring. They both believed strongly in higher education.

My mother had an understated elegance that I only realized after she passed when viewing her wardrobe and hearing stories from friends and family. My father was a dashing bachelor and dressed to impress. Both of my parents survived the Holocaust through their own treacherous journeys and met in Boyle Heights over a broken tube in a television set. My mother appreciated my father's dexterity and thought this skill would come in handy in their life adventures of love, marriage, and family. Once they were married, my mother chose to stay at home and take care of her family, while my father, without a college degree, taught himself electronic engineering and computer science. In addition to owning a bar and a TV repair service, my father's career included working at NASA's Jet Propulsion Laboratory (JPL) and he helped build Voyager-I that was launched on its interstellar mission in 1977.

In Memoriam

My father passed away 25 years ago, and in December 2020, my mother gently passed into the next world surrounded by family on a Saturday afternoon.

Mom and Dad, I love you both and miss you very much. This book and its teachings emanate from your love and tenacity to not only survive but thrive in times of adversity as well as in times of prosperity.

ACKNOWLEDGEMENTS

I wish to thank my sons Itzchak and Zachary for bringing joy into my life. They have given me inspiration to complete this book so that children and grown-up children everywhere can neutralize any traumas they may experience in their lives.

My parents, Michael (zt"l) and Lillian, without whom this work simply would not be. To my brother Harvey, your insight has been invaluable.

My clients, who entrusted and continue to entrust me with the most vulnerable aspects of themselves.

Special thanks goes to my editor Rivka Wolchin and assistant editors James Crewe, Alaina Snyder, Alina Demeter Esq, Shelley Tzorfas, and Vivian Eisenstadt MAPT CPT MASP, for their ability to convert my ramblings into the ideas and concepts you are reading. Thanks also to Adam Markey for his illustrations.

FOREWORD

I am pleased to take this opportunity to tell you about my friend and holistic healing colleague, Dr. Jeffrey Benton, and his book, Emotional Trauma Release Technique™: The Ultimate System for Releasing Life Traumas. I've known Dr. Benton for several years and I know him to be a compassionate, caring practitioner. Dr. Benton is not the average chiropractor. His interest in the well-being of the *whole* person led him on a quest to find ways of getting to the emotional core of physical pain. His Emotional Trauma Release Technique (ETRT) is the result of this quest.

No one could have written this book but Dr. Jeffrey Benton. You might say Dr. Benton, himself, was his very first patient, having endured devastating trauma in his own life and traveling a long, arduous journey toward achieving his own emotional healing. Dr. Benton's ETRT evolved from experiencing that personal journey, along with extensive research.

As holistic health practitioners, we realize that although Western medicine undeniably serves an important function in many instances of illness and injury, western medicine alone is simply not enough. Dr. Benton knew that chiropractic alone wasn't enough, either. Drugs may temporarily dull pain but beneath the drug-induced relief, emotional scars can continue to damage our musculoskeletal system, our organs, and our very cells.

Foreword

The human body is sensitive to chemical changes caused by emotional trauma. Unchecked, such trauma can manifest in a myriad of debilitating physical pains. Only when the source of the trauma is recognized and released and the physical pain abates, can one be free to truly experience joy in life.

If you suffer from longstanding physical pain that traditional modern medicine has not been able to alleviate, pain that perhaps chiropractic has helped but not eliminated, you are probably thinking, "Yeah, release the trauma and lose the pain sounds easy to say but it would take a miracle to do that for me!" If this is you, I urge you to read the testimonials from some of Dr. Benton's clients at the back of this book. These are just a small sampling of people struggling with pain that plagued them day and night who have gone to Dr. Benton. With ETRT, they have left his office with virtually a new lease on life. Releasing trauma and overcoming physical pain does not take a miracle—it takes Dr. Benton's Emotional Trauma Release Technique.

If you are looking at the prospect of having to take pain medication for the rest of your life, you owe it to yourself to read this book. Dr. Benton has been where you are as far as needing to overcome emotional trauma. He wrote this book because he truly cares about what you are going through. Dr. Benton believes God gifted this knowledge to him, and his mission is to share it with you. If your pain has left you wondering which way to turn for help, keep turning the pages of this book... you will find answers here!

Cherilyn Lee, PhD, NP, PA, RN, DD, holistic healer
Founder of NuWellnessHealthcare.com
Author of "Written Before I Was Born"
Marina Del Rey, CA 2019

BLESSING

8-1-21 ב"ה

Dr. Jeffrey Benton,

    I commend you on your continued pursuit to improve the health and well-being of others. I have known you as a chiropractor for many years, and have only heard excellent things from your patients. They describe your demeanor as both kind and compassionate, and relate their significant improvement based on your holistic approach.

    You are in a unique position to undertake this pursuit based on both your personal and professional journey. For this reason it is important, now more than ever, to help others address these needs when other approaches fail to do so.

    I wish you continued success as you complete your new book, <u>The Emotional Trauma Release Technique.</u> I bless you and those in need to find meaning in your book to help with the emotional and spiritual elements in their lives.

Sincerely,

Judge Rabbi Yuval Noff

ב"ה "מכתב - ברכה" 8-1-21

שויתי ה' לנגדי תמיד

לכבוד ידיד נפשי ולו"ר - לידידי את חברי היקר שהוא מחשוב הקהלה בעלי שלנו ועוד
Jeffrey Benton שי'

חיים טובים אלו - מחלת הקורונה רח"מנא לצלן, רוא איור ספרו החדש והאחרון
Emotional Trauma Release Technique

וידו רתה אמונה בראותי ספרו אשר חתכתה, בינה, ודעת,
ספר חשוב בזה פועלת רבים והלוקים הקורום "סיטואיצות רמלואות, ובדבר
הוא מאבל "רדיונות הלוקים". ובזה הוא אשר כיסיונות מיותרות של לחתגל
חיים חלולים עם בני דנוי משלחת,
בצלמונות מיותרות ולפצעות-תולוגות אחר ואות אל הדרך "אצלות - לשלל היד".

כמשה: כל לחתגל שקלי יסוד ביו' לעוב-ליבוב, זיך-לפני-וליאשר,
ומצביר בדאי "ואשלם" לו זה חחבר-הדבר אצלונו על פת היום, והיה",
ברמזם בהלח וחולה בה אמחתי אתנסו ויזין סעינוס יקפס אשר לו על רידיו התחלות
ובדבר ראשי שאת העמ ההלולים הדולום הבאו "הרמב"ם". בדרך לימוני דסתרו את הבוא

כן לעצם-ויש,
והלתחבר אשר הסודרית-אהובת-לשלם ליגרה על לשל וחולות כסוגר "של הבית
וחמצאים, ספר חשוב מאד יותן דה לחולת רבה אתרמצצים - הקשים - הם הפלוי"
וראיה הבידה גם בחלומים מעלה, ונה גם כל מפורש שלה אתרי מחלה זו לעצם ריגוי חיה החלוי
לכם, השלוחות המלול מזה לחמאל שי"ן

בברכה לחתם לבון מוקים שגאולים הקהולה ולידי ולדי דלילות חול, ו"ן
ולסגורם ריגוש זה "לבסמורם", "בשלוה אתתים, והצלחה ליציר ומתל הבריך

בברכת השנה
הפרכת הכב ילדוע' גל ואת ה'
דועוכ' ק'ל שאתה בתקמי
R.C.A

PREFACE

In my practice I treat individuals who have endured trauma in many of its forms—whether emotional, chemical, or physical. I have witnessed that, with time, the external wounds may heal, the effects of the non-visible types of trauma remain deep-rooted within the emotional center of the body, for weeks, months, years, or even lifetimes. We have yet to truly measure the long-term effect of such traumas on an individual and how these disassociation fragments, discussed later, affect their ability to function normally in society.

For instance, Post-Traumatic Stress Disorder (PTSD) is not limited to our men and women in uniform. It also negatively impacts anyone who has encountered emotional, sexual, physical, or verbal abuse, whether experienced once or for a prolonged period.

It has taken me over fifteen years to gather the material for this book. My goal of this book is to convey the knowledge with which the Creator has blessed me with and I have utilized in my practice. I apologize for the delay and invite you to join me in exploring how we can clear up our pasts so that we may live fully in the present, and create an exceptional future.

This book will help you understand how to clear emotional blockages that have been getting in your way, potentially hindering your

Preface

connection to your higher self, so that you can have a fulfilling relationship with yourself and others.

If you are reading this book, it likely that you are searching for a way to heal your past traumas and/or a broken heart. Or perhaps you are desiring to help someone in need of this work. Most people tend to learn from stories, and the stories and case studies I share with you in this book are true. ETRT is a great technique that will help you understand how to clear emotional blockages that have been getting in your way so that you can improve your connection to yourself and improve your relationships with others.

INTRODUCTION

In my 20 plus years in the field of healing, I have treated individuals who have endured emotional, chemical, or physical traumas in many of its forms. I have personally witnessed that even though, with time, the external wounds may have healed, the effects of the non-visible trauma remain. They can remain within the body for lifetimes, or even generations.

Medical science is only now beginning to take an accurate measure of how pervasive trauma exists within society. Post-Traumatic Stress Disorder (PTSD) has found its way to front-page headlines. Although doctors have tried to address the PTSD experiences of our veterans, they also need to address the PTSD effects of daily life. Even before the pandemic, previous surveys on teen mental health showed an increase in problems even before the pandemic hit. The percentage of teenagers saying they had persistent feelings of sadness or hopelessness rose from 26% in 2009 to 37% in 2019. The new survey had 44% saying they felt that way in 2021.[i] Post-Traumatic Stress Disorder can affect anyone, at any age, who has experienced emotional, sexual, physical, or verbal abuse, be it once or over a prolonged period of time.

This book is about showing you, the reader, that a life of joy and contentment can be yours.

Introduction

My Personal Journey

The Emotional Trauma Release Technique was developed as a result of a devastating break-up I experienced in my 30's. Now, as I look back at the pain and turmoil I experienced then, I can see clearly how the roots of my demise actually began before I was born.

I am the middle child of parents who were born in Czechoslovakia, now called the Czech Republic. My parents miraculously lived through the Holocaust (1938–1945). During that time, my parents, who had not yet met each other, separately witnessed and experienced unimaginable depravity of life. They saw systematic murder, desecration of human values, and total lack of respect for the human spirit.

They never knew if they would live to see the light of another day. The tremendous anxiety they endured, wondering if they would have their heads kicked in by a Nazi boot, is unimaginable.

My parents were held captive in several concentration camps, including Auschwitz-Birkenau. In 1945, my mother was liberated from a munitions factory in Bremberg, Germany. My parents met each other in Los Angeles after the war and got married in 1961.

It is difficult for us to fathom the enormous degree to which living through this traumatic experience impacted their lives. Witnessing horrific, catastrophic atrocities could never be forgotten, no matter how deeply they pushed them into their subconscious.

My parents' overwhelming fear of the unknown (not knowing if they were going to live or die during the holocaust) permeated our home with "anxious energy," making it difficult for me to stay focused. The psycho-emotional impact of what they endured was transferred to the family by invisible threads of uneasiness. This would express itself as me being unable to sit still; instead I would rock back and forth.

As a child I was unaware of the pall of anxiety and suffering that carried over from my parents' past. My older brother, my younger sister, and I were bathed in this nervous family atmosphere, which we mistook for normal. Initially, I could not identify the effects of my upbringing; I could only feel the effects of my experience. I questioned why I—a tall, attractive, college-educated professional—did not have many friends, and why I could not maintain a relationship. I was always antsy, could not stand still, and felt a constant need to pace around.

In my youth, I was forever seeking to understand what makes us behave the way we do. I was also fascinated by the human body and loved fixing broken things. In retrospect, it seems that it was natural for me to have put these two passions together. Both are about how I can make the body and spirit better, and help them function with poise. Following my instincts, and angelic guidance, I moved towards a career in healing. I trained to become a licensed chiropractor.

My Heart Broken Open

In my 30's, I dated a very special woman whom I believed to be a soul mate. While working in a chiropractic office I met an acupuncturist. We began working together, which led to dating. She felt the magical connection between us before I did. Our relationship continued for five years. Unfortunately I was blind to the reality of

Introduction

how deep and spiritual our connection actually was. It was only after we had broken up that I realized what I had lost.

Dating a soul mate sounds like reaching the pinnacle of connection, yet there were difficult times along the way. The Talmud says: "*To match couples together is as difficult as the splitting of the sea.*" (Sota 2A) I believe that while they are drawn together by some universal attraction, soul mate relationships are destined to have more challenges than do most prosaic relationships. Soul mate relationships are hard work. When one merits a soul mate it is because they are ready to be real and grow. Each mate helps the other evolve and elevate spiritually.

Pit of Despair

I did not appreciate how special this relationship was until it was too late. The lady in question, however, did. She felt a magical connection, and waited several years for me to feel it as well. We went to a therapist to discuss our relationship. At this meeting I told her that I did not feel any great connection. This was devastating news for her and, while walking away from that session, we agreed that we should end our relationship.

Literally 24 hours later, I woke up with a crushing feeling. It was as if something really heavy had crushed my spirit. I realized it was the loss of her love. I called her crying, and let her know how much I actually felt for her. But from her point of view, this was 24 hours too late. She told me she had been seeing someone else as friends, and had accepted his invitation to date after our therapy session.

I pursued her with romance, giving her flowers and "love is..." cut-outs from the newspaper, as well as inviting her to holiday dinners. We still saw each other at the chiropractic office, and were cordial at best.

I realized that I had not been as nurturing and devoted to her and her children as I should have been. I allowed my own limiting beliefs and anxieties to get in the way. My heartbreak was a catalyst to several personal awakenings. I realized that I truly loved her, and this forced me to deal with my broken heart and other issues. My meltdown was so tumultuous that I could have ended up at a psychiatric ward or worse had I not taken classes, attended prayer connections, and made use of other spiritual tools offered at the Kabbalah Centre in Los Angeles. There, I learned many empowering ways to raise my consciousness and transform my life through intention, prayer, and meditation.

As I cried to God for help to heal my aching heart and soul, I also asked for tools to help my soul mate heal her emotional wounds. I knew that I had to rebuild trust with her and her children to even have the possibility of re-establishing the magical connection that was broken between us.

This was no small task. During this period of healing and self-discovery, I realized my cultural view at that time was that I desired to find a single woman with no baggage (which I interpreted as someone who does not have children). This wonderful woman had two children, whom I subconsciously chose to label as not desirable, instead of embracing an opportunity to be part of their lives.

Introduction

As I look back, I recognize that I had been asleep and ignorant of this beautiful light in my life, which I eventually lost. By the time I awoke from my oblivion, it was too late.

Angelic Help

One afternoon, while I was at my apartment, I heard hundreds of voices (which I believe to be angels) screaming into my head, telling me that she was engaged. I freaked out and ran downstairs, not knowing what to do. I looked down, and in the gutter I saw three rings: A butterfly ring and two others. I knew that this was a sign that I needed to do something. If I wanted her I needed to propose marriage to her and her two children—hence the three rings. I grabbed the rings, cleaned them up, drove over to her home and told her that she could not marry this other person; that I loved her and I wanted to marry her. I gave her the butterfly ring. She was in shock, not just because I had proposed to her, but because how could I know? The other man had just proposed to her earlier that day! All of a sudden she had two proposals. Needless to say she was at her own crossroads. She eventually chose to not commit to either, deciding rather to focus on her children.

This time was especially painful on my heart. A few weeks later, I had fallen asleep at my apartment to the songs of ABBA, only to awaken at 5AM with tears gushing down my face and my heart painfully on fire. It felt as if rusted iron leaves covering up my heart were pushed open, exposing the vulnerable heart chakra beneath. It was an out-of-this-world sensation.

Emotional Trauma Release Technique

A moment later, at 5:01 AM, the phone rang. I picked it up and heard her sobbing. She was crying just as painfully and hard as I was. We both expressed our heartfelt love for each other and the synchronous agony we both felt, which was only for each other. We were on the phone for an hour, crying and sobbing, expressing our love for each other.

We met up shortly thereafter, and we went for a little walk holding each other's hands. It felt to me like we were not walking on the ground but instead floating on air. We did not say a word to each other and were just present together, experiencing this bliss.

She eventually broke up with the other person she was dating. We got back together and began working together again. I felt that I had grown since we had first broken up but obviously there was still more to do. Even though we knew we were soul mates, earthly laws also prevailed. Personal and professional differences began wedging their way between us.

There is a well-known saying: "Physician, heal thyself." This experience forced me to look at myself and examine who I was. My classes at the Kabbalah Centre, combined with the many healing modalities that I had studied at Chiropractic College, helped me elevate my consciousness to a higher vibration. I was finally able to stand still in a relaxed pose. I no longer felt that "anxious energy" which had plagued my childhood. The symbiotic relationship of hurtful heartbreak and healing became apparent. After much time and effort, the Emotional Trauma Release Technique was revealed to me.

The Neurobiology of Trauma

Trauma, according to the American Psychological Association (www.apa.org), is "an emotional response to a terrible event like an accident, rape or natural disaster."

Ruth Buczynski Ph.D. of the National Institute for the Clinical Application of Behavioral Medicine (NICABM), developed *The Neurobiology of Trauma* video series and interviewed several experts in this field. Here is a summary of relevant facts to help us understand how trauma affects all aspects of our body, nervous system and psyche.

Trauma

In the interview series, Bill O'Hanlon, LMFT, describes trauma as something that overwhelms a person's current resources, with predictable after effects. For example, one after effect is a disintegration (a disconnection); what he calls a "frozen in time" response neurologically, emotionally, relationally, and cognitively.

Some trauma is so extreme that people become catatonic. Bill O'Hanlon says, "There was a client who, when she remembered her trauma, would just 'black out.' Her explanation later was that she would go to a place where she did not feel anything, see anything, hear anything, and she wasn't in existence. She felt safe because nothing existed."

After a traumatic event, shock and denial are typical. Other reactions include unpredictable emotions, flashbacks, emotional outbursts, strained relationships and even physical symptoms like headaches or nausea. Some people have difficulty moving on with their lives.

Today, trauma is everywhere you look—on street corners, the interstate, in the news, and even in our homes. So what do we do? Do we hold up our hands to ward off the blow or crouch under something in fear? Neither of these options will empower us to take control of our situation.

The Scream

I came across a painting that made a big impression on me, called _The Scream_ (1893), by the Norwegian painter Evdard Munch. This painting shows a genderless figure in the foreground with its mouth open in a shout or scream, clutching its head with its hands. The background is also pretty evocative with its angry oranges and reds, and lines swirling around the isolated figure. As if to further emphasize the isolation there is a couple walking in the background who seem to have no connection with the main figure.

The Scream shouts trauma. The figure is suffering, oblivious to anyone around to comfort it. Its pain is not acknowledged. My thought was: *is the trauma the figure is experiencing emotional or physical, or a bit of both?*

The Scream (1893),
by the Norwegian artist
Edvard Munch.
~Wiki Commons

Modern Medicine:
A Nuanced Approach

Emotional trauma either manifests immediately or years later as chronic pain and/or disease. I believe that modern medicine's solution is to medicate these ailments by prescribing synthetic drugs made in a laboratory. Too often, modern medical practitioners subscribe to "numerous drugs as a fix all" philosophy, which mostly masks the symptoms. A painful example is the over-prescription of opiate drugs and the resultant opiate dependency. Medicine definitely has its place in health and wellness, but not at the expense of the health or wealth of the patient. As we are seeing, this "opioid epidemic" has become a leading health crisis and continually shows the spiraling consequences of trying to fix a symptom (pain) that often leads to addiction, poorer health outcomes, and in the worst cases—death.

In my opinion, there are times when synthetic drugs are not the solution. Synthetic medications often simply mask the problem and do not get at the underlying cause. I am not trying to undermine the medical profession as it does bring a lot of good, especially in cases of acute trauma and medical emergencies. I am speaking more to the long-term care of those suffering with chronic diseases.

Some social observers have alleged that medical over-prescribing is at the behest of the big pharmaceutical companies. Doctors, these critics allege, push pills on patients as a way to ensure profits. I do not want to delve down the rabbit hole of conspiracy, but handing out pills for every ailment is no solution. We definitely should not be doping up our children, for this in turn can create life-long drug dependency. We were not put on Earth to live pill to pill, capsule to capsule!

At the Light Touch Healing Center, we define trauma as a deeply disturbing or distressing experience that can disrupt the body, mind, and soul's ability to function optimally. Traumatic events may damage our lives temporarily or permanently. They can leave us feeling distressed, vulnerable, alone, and give us the sense of clinging to a rock while dark waters seem to rise.

Trauma and Dissociation

In an interview with Dr. Ruth Buczynski in the video series *The Neurobiology of Trauma,* Dr. Dan Siegel, an internationally recognized educator, practicing child psychiatrist and author of several books, including Mindsight: The New Science of Personal Transformation, explains that trauma causes peri-traumatic dissociation—when people dissociate at the time the trauma occurs—and is the biggest risk factor for developing Post-Traumatic Stress Disorder (PTSD). He says, "With dissociation, the sense of self is profoundly assaulted. Dissociation itself becomes traumatizing. Because if you cannot rely on your own experiences, then your own sense of self is itself a cause of being overwhelmed by things."

Dr. Buczunski continues that the outcome of a dissociative response will be impaired integration, which is one of the hallmarks of a traumatized brain. A traumatized brain is an unbalanced brain, resulting in an unbalanced nervous system. An unbalanced nervous system blocks our capacity for flexible, adaptive, and stable functioning, thus blocking proper memory integration.

Dr. Siegel further explains that developmental attachment research has shown that disorganized attachment is at least one of the precursors to people experiencing dysfunctional forms of dissociation. Disorganized attachment occurs when stimuli come at us from an experience, that we need to take and place within all aspects of our nervous system. This overwhelms the nervous system and causes dissociation fragments.

When we are unable to integrate memory—if we are not able to take the separate pieces and put them together in an explicit form—this can wreak havoc on a person's internal sense of coherence and adds another layer of anxiety on an already tense situation. This can wind out of control leading to a mental breakdown. When stress is chronic or we constantly relive trauma, we struggle to bounce back.

Further in the *Neurobiology of Trauma* series by Ruth Buczynski PhD, Dr. Stephen Porges—author of the *Polyvagal Theory* and distinguished University Scientist at the Kinsey Institute, Indiana University, and Professor of Psychiatry at the University of North Carolina—says "Basically, the nervous system is adjusting to those demands without the normal periods of recovery and rejuvenation."

The Emotional Trauma Release is the bridge to help decrease the anxiety and calm the erratic nervous mind. ETRT can mean the difference between a life of ongoing pain, anxiety, and stress, versus a life of physical wellbeing, emotional security, and tranquility.

Unexpected or Shock Trauma

The Emotional Trauma Release Technique (ETRT) is a natural healing modality that helps us neutralize and disconnect our behavioral reactions from past or present emotional and/or physical events.

Most of the time, we associate trauma as extremely stressful emotional or physical events that disrupt the body's ability to function and process normally. These types of events shatter our sense of security, making us feel vulnerable. The most common form of trauma are those unexpected situations that leave us feeling flabbergasted or shocked. A near-miss car accident, the unexpected violent shaking of an airplane, a slamming door, startle us.

However, it is not the physical act alone that determines whether an event is psychologically traumatic. It is our **Subjective Emotional Filter** that will dictate how we emotionally experience each event.

The more frightened and helpless we feel in any given situation, the more likely we are to be traumatized, causing our psyche to store the event as a negative experience. Over time, negative memories persist at both the conscious and subconscious levels. This results in adverse emotional and physical consequences.

Many studies have demonstrated the negative effect of emotional stress on a wide range of health issues, including cardiovascular disease, chronic stress, digestive disorders, and even cancer.[1,2,3] The solution to ending this cycle is to disconnect from the program and simply turn it off. But how do we do that?

Case Study: Joel

Joel, a busy executive in his mid-30s, was having a casual lunch when he got injured while eating his meal. He had ordered a shish kebab, which was prepared on an open flame and held in place with skewers. Unbeknownst to him, when the food was plated, a piece of the wooden skewer broke off and remained lodged in the food. While Joel was eating his kebab, the broken spike stabbed the roof of his mouth, piercing his oral cavity and gashing blood vessels. Needless to say, he was bleeding profusely and had to be rushed to the local emergency room to get medical attention.

After this unfortunate event, Joel was so traumatized that he developed an aversion to toothpicks, any type of speared food, restaurants and servers. He would become anxious whenever he ordered food. Joel recalled a moment where he blew up at a waiter who had innocently delivered sliders with toothpicks in them. He literally yelled at the server to remove the food. He would not have reacted this way had he not sustained injury to his upper palate.

Joel suffered what I call an emotional and physical trauma as a result of his restaurant experience. This quickly developed into a fixation that became stored in his auric emotional body. To help better understand this concept, in her book, _Light Emerging: The Journey of Personal Healing_, Barbara Ann Brennan explains the auric emotional body. She credits Dr. Victor Inyushin of the Kazakh University in Russia as explaining that there is a fifth state of matter that is different from the other four states—solids, liquids, gases, and plasma—called bio-plasma." Brennan describes this bio-plasma as seven levels of the human energy field. Each level penetrates through the body and extends outward from the skin. Each successive level is of a higher frequency from the preceding level. These seven levels, known as Auric Fields, each correspond to a different level of life experience.

She adds that our emotional body is the second closest aura to our physical body and affects our psyche. This phenomenon of stored emotional traumas allows us to go about our lives in a normal fashion until something triggers one of these stored packages of memories, causing it to explode. I call this phenomenon **"emotional land-mines."**

In Joel's situation, he did not necessarily understand how this aversion to restaurants developed. Subconsciously it was created by his body's defense mechanism to protect him from the danger of being stabbed in his mouth. His emotional body had created a belief in him that no food preparer is safe. In time, Joel began preparing his own food at home, rarely eating out.

As is often the case, physical and emotional traumas are closely connected with one another. When Joel visited the Light Touch Healing Center, he explained that he was feeling tense. He was the victim of a single traumatic experience that seemed to overtake his life. He had been feeling paralyzed with fear and felt like he had lost his ability to move confidently in the day-to-day world. He was also experiencing pain in his neck, which he felt was built-up tension.

Joel and I talked the matter over and retraced his steps, back to the day of the skewer incident. Then we applied the Emotional Trauma Release Technique. Joel began to feel better and the pain in his neck subsided. Once again, he began once again to live without fear. He recovered his edge and self-confidence. Joel was once again able to socialize and returned to eating out at restaurants.

Trauma

Notes

Chapter Two:

Stress

"Identify your problems but give your power and energy to solutions."

~ Tony Robbins

൚൚

According to the Oxford Dictionary, stress can be described as "a state of mental or emotional strain, resulting from adverse or very demanding circumstances," and a stressor as "something that causes a state of strain or tension." Yet stress is also known to be essential for survival because the chemicals triggered by stress help the body prepare to face imminent danger.

In ancient times, quick reactions to unexpected situations was the difference between life and death. (It used to be so much simpler for ancient humans!) They lived in a time of survival, essentially providing for themselves and their family's physiological needs and safety. They roamed the alluvial plains by day, seeking food, and fending for themselves against an array of scary creatures. When being chased by a bear or saber-toothed tiger, in addition to direct sympathetic nervous system activation, the natural fight or flight hormones and chemicals were released, helping to save their lives.

A simple explanation of how this process works is understanding our autonomic nervous system, which is comprised of both a sympathetic and parasympathetic nervous system. In response to stress, the sympathetic nervous system kicks in. There is a direct connection from the eye to the mid-brain. This allows for a millisecond response to a threat. The specific area is called the periaqueductal gray (PAG) region of the mid-brain. In addition to stimulation to this area of the brain, the hormone adrenaline is released. Blood is shifted to the muscles and away from the stomach and other organs; pupils become dilated.

The stimulated sympathetic nervous system also activates secretion of cortisol releasing hormone in the brain. Cortisol is then released from the adrenal glands, causing sugar and triglycerides to be secreted into the blood stream to feed the muscle response. These hormones help skeletal muscles fire faster and more strongly, enhancing our senses. They enable us to run faster and/or use our muscles for defending ourselves if need be in a "fight or flight" situation.

There is also a parasympathetic activation known as the "freeze" response. In an emergency, the sympathetic nervous system prepares us to fight or flee, but if this behavior is perceived to be too dangerous, the parasympathetic nervous system puts on the brakes to stop us. Freezing is not a passive state but rather a parasympathetic brake on the motor system, relevant to perception and action preparation. In this state, people's muscles become limp and their metabolism shuts down. Even though both sympathetic and parasympathetic branches of the autonomic nervous system are simultaneously activated, in case of parasympathetic dominance do we observe defensive freezing. This is again mediated by the periaqueductal gray (PAG) matter in the mid-brain.

In modern times, although these same stress hormones are activated, the situation is vastly different. In our internet era, there are no saber-tooth tigers roaming the streets, thus many of the stressors of life tend to come from mental and emotional events we cannot simply fight or run from.

Our lives have become more complicated, high-paced, and intense than they were for our parents and grandparents. We are bombarded by so much information, especially since the advent of the smart phone, which allows immediate access to infinite amounts of input. Do not get me wrong; social media has much for which we should feel grateful, such as giving us the ability to connect with family and friends. However, the general stress of making ends meet is now coupled with personal competition as we are pushed to measure our self-worth not only by degrees of perfection like perfect weight, looks, and degrees on the wall. We are driven by how many "likes" and "followers" we get on Instagram, Facebook, Snapchat, Tik Tok, Twitter or whatever is currently popular.

People rarely visit one another anymore just to catch up. It is much more convenient to pick up the phone and text—yes I said text, not even call—our friends or loved ones. We rarely take time to relax, let alone vacation, as many of us are working more than one job just to make ends meet. We eat convenient packaged fast-foods instead of taking the time to enjoy cooking a wholesome meal from fresh ingredients.

Today, it is all about having things instantly, which puts enormous stress on us physically, emotionally, and spiritually. We go to work earlier and stay later. Our weekends are sucked away just trying to handle the chores we could not get to during the week. We have forgotten what it means just to breathe, relax, and enjoy life.

Advertising and social media marketing bombard us with images of how we should look, what we should buy, and how we should behave, targeting our unconscious need to be perfect and fit in. Something as significant as feeling inadequate creates internal turmoil causing stress-related hormones and chemicals to flood our body. However, instead of being metabolized by us using our body in some mechanical way (like running), these hormones and chemicals persist and circulate in higher concentrations inside our bodies. This results in all kinds of health problems, like high blood pressure, inflammation and autoimmune diseases.

In September 2018, the World Health Organization declared stress to be the "health epidemic of the 21st century." Chronic ongoing stress can damage a person's mind and body. The heart and circulation can also be affected. Anyone who has experienced that feeling of "butterflies" in their stomach knows what I mean. This is a case of stress interfering with a person's digestion.

Emotional Splinters

I would describe the stressors of modern life as "emotional splinters" that get under our skin and annoy us mercilessly. Over time, these emotional splinters can erode our instinctive ability to adapt, as well as constantly stimulate our central nervous and immune systems, which predisposes us to hypersensitivity and dis-ease. Sometimes we are so traumatized by an event that it feels like we have been stabbed with a dagger. An example of an emotional splinter not healing is presented in the case study below.

Case Study: Decreased Chronic Foot Pain

I met a woman sitting on a bench at the Pasadena Civic Center who told me that she was suffering with chronic pain in her foot, which was the result of a recent surgery. I detected an energy block (emotional splinter) around that foot and ankle region and asked her to breathe in while tilting her head back. Moments later, she reported that the pain had decreased from an eight to a four. The look of relief on her face spoke volumes. See the video here entitled "Dr. Jeffrey Benton - Clearing Post-Surgical Residual Foot Pain" https://youtu.be/kRSgNixdrp8

Stressors Have Memory

The part of the brain responsible for the perception of emotions such as anger, fear, sadness, and pleasure, as well as the controlling of aggression is called the amygdala. We remember stressful and traumatic events by pairing them with emotions, which, if we did not lock up, would make us feel stifled and potentially too traumatized to move. We would not be able to function. However, locking up these emotions in our subconscious sucks up our Life-Force energy. We need to divert some of our daily fuel charge, which would normally have gone toward physical and brain activity, to now managing this task of keeping traumatic memories at bay.

The downside of storing stressors in our subconscious rather than processing them is the physical manifestations of pain, depression, anxiety, apathy, and overall exhaustion. Emotional memories endure whether we are aware of them or not. In my opinion, the saying, "time heals all wounds," is simply make-believe. In fact, emotions that are not dealt with and neutralized manifest as energetic frequencies that persist and are visible on a Functional MRI (fMRI).

The amygdala helps us to process and store memories of events and emotions so that an individual may be able to recognize similar events in the future. When someone thinks of a past situation that invokes either anger, grief, excitement, or joy, this causes different areas of the brain to light up. Professor of Communication and Psychology, Dr. Ross Buck reports: "We now have the opportunity to actually see how the brain is reacting to emotional stimuli, and things that were previously hidden are now observable and measureable."[4] See brain fMRI images below depicting grief, joy, rage and fear.[5]

Expression and suppression of emotions is called Emotion Regulation. For the scientific minded, studies point to the medial prefrontal cortex and the amygdala in the brain as the organs responsible for Emotional Regulation. The processes of regulation of emotion trigger activation of the ventromedial prefrontal cortex and inhibition of the amygdala.[6]

Biological models of PTSD propose that reduced medial prefrontal cortex (MPFC) activity leads to impaired inhibition over the amygdala fear processing networks, resulting in amygdala hyper-responsiveness. An example is severe rage or severe depression.

Dr. Sebern Fisher, author of *Neurofeedback in the Treatment of Developmental Trauma*, notes that fear circuits are in the temporal lobe and that survival's fear circuit—"the survival amygdala"—is in the right hemisphere.

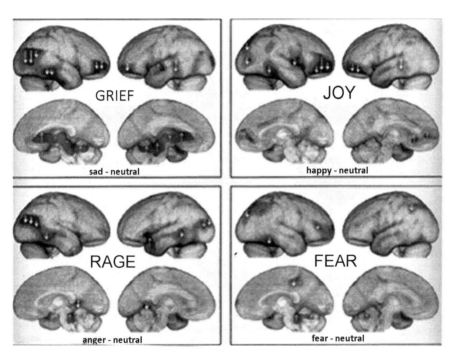

The amygdala is the organ devoted to keeping emotions alive. One reason chronic pain persists is because a thought pattern in the amygdala is switched on that says, "I need to feel pain in order to survive."

Neurofeedback Therapy vs ETRT

Advances in trauma therapy allow us to see neural activity in the brain in real time. These advances utilize Electro-Encephalography (EEG) where sensors are placed on the head. These sensors detect the firing domain of the brain live, in real time. Patients can actively see what brainwaves their brain is producing by viewing them on a computer monitor. It is a mirror for the brain to be looking at its own activity.

The patient is, for the first time, able to train sites in the brain. Clinicians and researchers use this EEG technology to allow the patient to consciously create a brain wave frequency for a "quieting of fear," inhibiting those frequencies that get in the way of clear thinking or functioning.[7]

People with PTSD and traumatic brain injury (TBI) have slower wave activity in the brain and anxious people have faster wave activity. Neurofeedback therapy allows real time feedback via EEG as a tool so one can literally play a video game with their own brain to either inhibit the way slow wave activity (which normally occurs in sleep) or the very fast wave activity (which occurs when one is experiencing tension and anxiety) to get the brain to a relaxed state, which is when it makes Alpha waves. The circuit targeted by this therapy is in the temporal lobe of the right hemisphere because that is the part of the brain that is overactive, disorganized, and highly aroused. During the course of the video game, and over time, the person will feel more relaxed, and often their body will become heavy or slow as they shift into a para-sympathetic (relaxed) mode.

As seen in the diagram on the next page, there are specific brain wave frequencies that let us feel calmer and quieter. We want to train the brain to get in touch with these frequencies.

Nature of Sine Wave Activity in the Brain	Frequency Level & Description
(high frequency waveform)	**BETA 14 – 30 Hertz** Awake, normal levels of alertness. Also associated with overactive thinking patterns, stress, anxiety, frustration and other undesired states. People spend most of their daily life operating at this level.
(medium frequency waveform)	**ALPHA 9 – 13 Hertz** Relaxed, calm levels of mental activity occur at this level. A peaceful state associated with tranquillity and relaxation, which people can achieve through effective relaxation exercises and meditation.
(lower frequency waveform)	**THETA 4 – 8 Hertz** A deeper state of mindfulness associated with creative insight, cognitive & memory enhancement and feelings of deep connectedness. Also the level at which people naturally progress into sleep state.
(very low frequency waveform)	**DELTA 1 – 3 Hertz** The deepest brainwave level associated with dreamless (non-REM) sleep. Essential for proper restoration of health and immune system. Difficult to achieve this level if overactive at the Beta level.

There are two kinds of training in Standard Neurofeedback:

1) Eyes open—training the brain to make more Alpha waves, while playing a video game

2) Eyes closed—training the brain to make more Alpha-Theta waves while generally lying down. The feedback is primarily auditory, for example, listening to the sound of the ocean.

One of the premises when working with pathological conditions is that it may be easier to reach the mind through regulating the brain than it is to regulate the brain through mind practices. Neurofeedback helps the brain learn to regulate itself. As a result, destructive reactions fall away and mindfulness is enhanced.

A distinction between neurofeedback and ETRT is that neurofeedback trains the brain to create certain frequencies, and ETRT *neutralizes* the physiological-emotional reaction between the trauma and how it was perceived and stored in the brain.

Emotional Landmines: Tentacles of Emotional Triggers

Mines are destructive devices placed on land or at sea that are designed to explode when they are touched. In my practice, I coined the phenomenon of the **Emotional Landmine**, depicted below, as a trigger device surrounding the heart with long arms or tentacles. Each arm has several emotional receptors, and each receptor is tuned to a past traumatic event. Like those stealthy devices of destruction, you never know when you are going to trigger an Emotional Landmine. When you do, it seemingly comes from nowhere. A lazy handheld stroll in the park with a significant other suddenly comes to an abrupt halt because of a glance at someone else or an ill-timed or ill-stated comment. This Emotional Landmine is tethered to a person's psyche as illustrated by the chain.

The comedienne, Lynne Koplitz, describes how the innocuous act of leaving a sock on the living room floor can evolve into an emotional "tornado" in her Netflix comedy special *Hormonal Beast*. Whereas a hurricane you can prepare for, since it is tracked. A tornado comes suddenly; there is no preparation, and it most often destroys everything.

ETRT assists the body's healing process by identifying stored emotional memories in the auric emotional body, identifying their root cause, and neutralizing these minefields within the body and psyche. These emotional minefields have really long energetic receptors that are on constant alert, waiting to be triggered by similar conditions or circumstances that originally led to their formation. As clients tap into the trapped emotions that are locked inside these minefields, they often feel an intense, overwhelming sensation like something is exploding inside them. Their bodies may begin to shudder and shake uncontrollably. They may cry, deep heartfelt sobs. As these emotions begin bubbling to the surface, there is a physical release as they exit the body. This is a very real and vivid experience for them.

Stress

Notes

Chapter Three:

Emotions

"Holding onto anything is like holding onto your breath. You will suffocate."

~ Deepak Chopra

Where Emotions are Stored

I believe that when we encounter traumatic events, the energies created by that stressor first settle in our musculoskeletal system. Our muscles become tense, sometimes making it hard to breathe; we may even feel pain in our chest or experience migraines.

There are times when it is not safe to verbalize or act on our truth in the moment. For example, in the case of a victim of a robbery being held at gunpoint, it is not the smartest survival skill to fight back in the moment. It is probably better for this individual to relinquish their physical belongings. At this point in their mind, they can choose either to commend themselves for making the best choice possible,

Emotions

given the circumstances or they can beat themselves up for not being able to defend themselves and fight off the attacker.

The tremendous feelings associated with the emotional trauma experienced in an event like that described above need to be alleviated for complete healing to take place. Unfortunately these feelings (the energy) rarely get cleared at all. The effect of the trauma tends to get stored short-term in the muscles of the head, neck, and shoulders. And the sufferer often describes what they have gone through using words like: rage, shame, and dread, which disempowers all the aspects of the human being—body, mind, and spirit.

Ancient Chinese medicine describes how bio-plasma, also known as Qi (Chi) or energy, travels the entire body through energy channels called "meridians." Unresolved traumatic effects can get stored long-term in the meridians.

Acupuncturists are accustomed to treating long-term emotional trauma. They are trained in pulse-taking and can gauge the quality of the energy coursing through these meridians. They know that disease processes begin when the Chi or Qi dynamic (flow of life force energy) of the meridians are disrupted by trauma.

There are two main Central Meridians that run up and down the middle of our body. One is the Governing Vessel, which runs from the base of the lower back (sacrum), up the spine, over

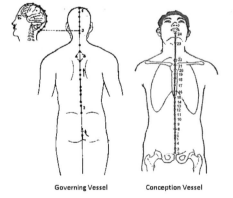

Governing Vessel   Conception Vessel

the skull, ending at the top of the upper lip. The other is called the Conception Vessel, which runs from the perineum up the front of the body, ending at a point just below the lower lip.

The Governing Vessel (GV) and Conception Vessel (CV) are of the same Life-Force energy source. They are inseparable and are known as the Yin-Yang, front-back duality. The two main emotional frequencies associated with these two meridians are: false pride (associated with the GV) and shame (associated with the CV). False pride is an exaggerated, pretentious opinion of oneself, one's abilities, or one's circumstance that is not based on real achievement or success. Shame is a painful feeling of humiliation caused by the misperception of a wrongful or foolish behavior perpetrated or experienced by the individual. For the purpose of this book, the feeling of shame occurs in response to an emotional traumatic event or the triggering of a previously emotional trauma event; and false pride sometimes occurs as a self-protective response to receiving continual emotional belittling.

These Central Meridians are the main portals that allow all the other emotions such as anger, sadness and grief, etc. to be stored in the body.

Sometimes, in the workplace or at home, we may experience an event that bothers us and throws our soul out of alignment. And even though we subconsciously know that what has occurred is not correct, we do not feel safe to express that truth and we pretend that things are okay when they really are not.

I have found that false pride and shame originate from a lack of nurturance. However, the feeling of shame comes from being unable to consciously acknowledge the truth in the moment. We tend to feel the emotion of shame later on; be it a day, a week, a year, a decade, a lifetime after the incident took place. The tragic truth is that if this trauma does not get cleared, it is imprinted epigenetically. This means that our children and/or our grandchildren and/or our great grandchildren and so on, have to deal with it.

Exodus 34:6-7 says: *"The Lord, God, merciful and gracious, long-suffering, and abundant in goodness and truth; keeping mercy to the thousandth generation, forgiving iniquity and transgression and sin; and that will by no means clear the guilty; visiting the iniquity of the fathers upon the children, and upon the children's children, to the third and to the fourth generation."*

Say, for example, our boss makes fun of us in front of the entire office. The truth is that although the comment was hurtful and we feel humiliated, standing up for ourselves is not the best option. Doing so might have dire financial and emotional consequences. Thus we keep quiet and pretend that how we have been humiliated does not bother us and instead put on a mask of "false pride."

In such a situation, if the issue we were confronted with does not get acknowledged, dealt with, and cleared, the traumatic event is stored somewhere in the meridian system until such time that processing can occur. The place where it gets stored is unique to each individual.

False pride is the expression of covering things up. Shame is when we try to ignore something and then it creeps out unexpectedly, often retriggered by a similar scenario or an Emotional Landmine.

The Frequency of Emotions

According to Lisa Feldman Barrett, PhD, a university distinguished Professor of Psychology at Northeastern University and author of *How Emotions are Made*, "We do not and cannot detect emotions in anybody, ever. This is because emotions are not what we think they are. They are not universally expressed and recognized. They are not hardwired brain reactions that are uncontrollable. It may feel to you like your emotions are hardwired, and they just trigger and happen to you, but they do not. You may believe that you are prewired, born with emotion circuits, but you are not. No brain contains emotion circuits. Emotions are guesses that your brain constructs in the moment, and you have more control over these guesses than you might imagine that you do.

"The bottom line is that emotions are not built into your brain at birth. They are just built. Using past experience, your brain predicts and constructs your experience of the world. We use past experience based on similar situations to try to make meaning. Emotions that we seem to detect in other people actually come in part from what is inside our own head.

"And so the lesson here is that emotions which seem to *happen* to you are actually *made* by you. You are not at the mercy of mythical emotional circuits buried deep inside some ancient part of your brain. You have more control over your emotions than you think you do.

Your brain is wired so that if you change the ingredients that your brain uses to make emotion, then you can transform your emotional life. This is what I call being the architect of your experience."[8]

When a life experience does not support our well-being, we are seldom conscious that **we have a choice** not to react and instead embrace this event as an opportunity to bring balance. Emotions that are not processed in the moment get stored in the body as emotional resonant frequencies. Everything in existence today has and vibrates at its own unique natural frequency. In the emotional realm, the same is true. Emotions vibrate at their own resonance frequencies, as per Dr. David Hawkins, author of *Power vs Force: The Hidden Determinants of Human Behavior*, and the German New Medicine developed by Dr. Ryke Geerd Hamer.

In his research, Dr. Hamer discovered that every disease, even a heart attack, stroke, or cancer, is controlled from its own specific area in the brain and linked to a very particular, identifiable, "conflict shock."[9] In the case of serious diseases like cancer, Dr. Hamer found that without exception he could trace the development of cancer to a severe emotional shock, especially one for which the person was totally unprepared. Furthermore, he discovered that every shock leaves a dark shadow on the brain, which was confirmed in every case by a brain scan. He also found that the exact nature of the shock or conflict determined the site for the disease. In other words, he found an exact correlation between the shadow on the brain, the location of disease in the body, and the specific type of unresolved conflict![10]

Exercise:

Think about the emotion of fear. What does it bring up for you? Where do you feel it in your body? How big is it? What is the sensation? Is there a color, smell or taste associated with it?

Now think about the emotion of grief. What does it bring up for you? Where do you feel it in your body? How big is it? What is the sensation? Is there a color, smell or taste associated with it?

As you will notice, fear and grief sit differently within you. They each have their own vibrational frequency, which I term an "emotional resonance response." ™

Map of Consciousness

In *Power Vs. Force: The Hidden Determinants of Human Behavior*, physician David R. Hawkins MD[11] describes using muscle testing to map out the logarithmic energies of different consciousness states. Hawkins calls this chart a "Map of Consciousness." Assigning values from 0 to 1000, Hawkins ascribes a number to identifiable states of consciousness. Below is a list of some examples:

- Shame vibrates at an energy of 20.
- Blame and guilt vibrate at an energy of 30
- Hopelessness and despair vibrate at an energy of 50
- Grief vibrates at an energy of 75
- Fear vibrates at an energy of 100
- Courage vibrates at energy of 200
- Trust vibrates at an energy of 250

Emotions

- Love vibrates at an energy of 500 (measured at 432hz)
- Peace vibrates at an energy of 600
- Enlightenment vibrates at an energy of 700-1000

We can sense these vibrational energies if we pay close attention. Think about how you feel when you are depressed or tired. Then think of how you feel when you trust someone or when you are in love with someone.

How Emotions Get Stuck and Overwhelm the Body

When an emotional or physical traumatic event occurs, we are startled, reflexively look up, and stop breathing. This simple action is the opening that allows the traumatic event to affect our psyche negatively and lower our Life-Force energetic vibration. If we are aware and entirely present to the event, we can separate ourselves and allow this energy to dissipate and not affect us.

Yet often times we are not cognizant of what is occurring because it is either not safe to emote and process what is happening or we do not know that we are being energetically traumatized, and we put up a false face in order to function and to conform to societal norms. The emotional trauma remains "buried" in our subconscious.

As a result, the energy of the traumatic event moves through the two Central Meridians, GV and CV, and lodges in the meridian specifically associated with that emotional frequency, causing an **Emotional Rut**—a never-ending trench.

This never-ending trench is where the emotions forever remain, slowly piling up and reducing one's excitement for life. If left unresolved, the body's Life-Force channels collapse, pressing the body to adapt to the stressors and reconfigure alternate, less efficient ways to receive and transmit energy.

Storage Warehouses of Unfinished Business

We go through life collecting and storing both emotional and physical trauma all over our body. These stored traumas wait until a time when they can be processed and resolved to completion. However, completion often does not occur, and these traumatic emotions pile up into what I call "Storage Warehouses of Unfinished Business."

Eventually our warehouse becomes so full that it explodes. When this happens we begin to feel achy, tired, run-down, anxious, and/or depressed. Doctors often call this old age; psychologists may call it emotional distress; I call it trauma overload.

Emotions

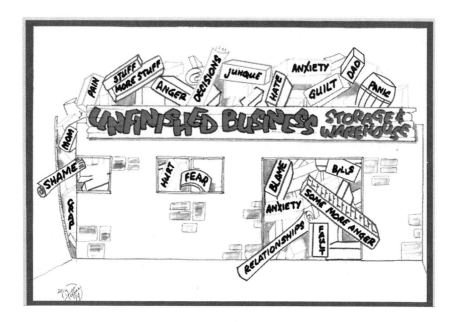

Adverse Child Experiences

This tipping point where vitality drops precipitously usually occurs after age thirty-five, but can occur at a very young age. The Centers for Disease Control (CDC) calls these traumas that occur in childhood Adverse Childhood Experiences (ACEs).

In one groundbreaking study combating obesity by researchers at the Kaiser Permanente San Diego Department of Preventive Medicine in the 1980s, it was reported that there was a high incidence of participants who dropped out of their obesity clinic. Dr. Vincent Felitti, the lead researcher of the study, was dumbfounded at this discovery.[12] This mystery began a 25 year quest, involving over 17,000 members of Kaiser Permanent's San Diego Care program.[13]

The first of their many counterintuitive discoveries was that the great majority of the dropouts (over 85%) actually were successfully losing weight with this program. When the researchers took detailed life interviews of the study participants, they unexpectedly revealed that childhood abuse was remarkably common and predated the onset of their obesity. Many patients spoke openly of an association between the two. The counterintuitive aspect was that, for many people, obesity was not their problem; it was their protective solution to problems that previously had never been discussed with anyone.

An early insight became evident when the memorable remark of a woman who was raped at age twenty-three and gained 105 pounds in the subsequent year: "Overweight is overlooked, and that's the way I need to be." The contrast was striking between this statement and her desire to lose weight. Similarly, two men who were guards at a state penitentiary became anxious after losing more than 100 pounds each. They made it clear that they felt much safer going to work looking "big as a refrigerator" instead of "normal size." Overall, the researchers found the simultaneous presence of opposing forces to be common; many of their weight program patients were driving with one foot on the brakes and one on the gas, wanting to lose weight but fearful of change.

Dr. Vincent Felitti writes that the ACE Study compared the current adult health status of these participants with eight categories of adverse childhood experience that were frequently identified in the weight program. Three categories pertained to personal abuse: recurrent physical abuse, recurrent emotional abuse, and sexual abuse. Four categories pertained to growing up in a dysfunctional household i.e. with an alcoholic person or a drug user; where someone was in prison; where someone was chronically depressed, mentally ill, or suicidal; where the mother was treated violently; and where the parents were separated, divorced, or in some way lost to the patient during childhood.

They found a common theme that being overweight had a protective effect on these individuals. In the case of a man who had been beaten up when he was a skinny kid, being overweight kept him safe because when he gained hundreds of pounds, no one bothered him. Another participant, this time female, shared that her father, while raping her when she was seven years old, told her that the only reason he was not doing the same to her nine-year-old sister was because her sister was fat. So logically her becoming obese protected her. This study found that losing weight increased their anxiety, depression, and fear to levels that were intolerable. In their minds, being slim made them vulnerable to re-experience the traumas they had as children.

According to the CDC, Adverse Childhood Experiences (ACE) are vastly *more* common than recognized or acknowledged, and "are one of the leading, if not the leading determinant of the health and social well-being of our nation."[14,15] Of equal importance was their observation that these experiences had a powerful correlation to adult health a half-century later. Slightly more than half of their middle-class population of Kaiser Permanente's Health Plan members experienced one or more of the categories studied. One in four was exposed to two categories of abusive experience, one in 16 to four categories. It was found that given an exposure to one category, there is an 80% likelihood of exposure to another. All this, of course, is well shielded by social taboos against obtaining this information. Further, one may "miss the forest for the trees" if one studies these issues individually. **They do not occur in isolation.** ACE's occur in clusters, and can contribute to high risk health behaviors like addiction and destructive behaviors in adulthood.

The question to ask is: How will these childhood experiences play out decades later in a doctor's office? How does one perform reverse alchemy, going from a normal newborn with almost unlimited potential (gold) to a diseased, depressed adult (lead)?

As gloomy as this sounds, there are techniques like ETRT to apply reverse alchemy, turning lead back into gold once again; rekindling a zest for life with stamina, joy, and unlimited potential.

Case Study: Date Rape Release

A young lady, whose identity will be kept anonymous, was referred to the Light Touch Healing Center for neuromuscular pain. She had been in psychiatric care for ten days at Cedar Sinai Hospital for significant concerns about her state of mind and whether she might be a danger to herself or to the community. The person referring this young lady to us explained that she was admitted because it was thought she had deliberately driven into the yellow barrels filled with water that buttress the freeway off ramp. However, the accident occurred because as she was making a left turn at a green light, another car's headlights blinded her and she crashed her car. This resulted in her experiencing psychosis.

I sat down with this young lady and gently assessed her with applied kinesiology. This process utilizes muscle testing to determine neurologic integrity of different body parts, which is explained in

Emotions

more detail later in this book. After checking her neck and upper body, I turned my attention to her legs. As I palpated her right thigh, while applying downward pressure to her left arm, the arm went weak, indicating something was wrong. Because I did not see any visible markings on her skin on the right thigh, I asked her if anything had happened to this area of her body. Her demeanor changed as she told me that she had been sexually assaulted while on a date. "That's where he grabbed me," she said. The assailant grabbed her by the thigh and pulled her down. I gently extended her head back an inch on her inhale breath and brought it back to neutral as she exhaled. We repeated this procedure a few times. The rest of the visit was focused on clearing all the different aspects that this date rape trauma effected: her heart, her trust in herself, in men, in God.

This single two hour visit shifted her life. She experienced relief from the physical ills, and explained that she also felt the release and removal of the emotional trauma and resultant blockages that had been driving her to distraction. She now could think clearly and felt a return of her power. No longer did she let that adverse event define her. She could return to her productive and positive life.

She wrote me a testimonial after that sesson. Below is an excerpt from this letter.

Last but not least, he didn't ask me for any rewards or payments; he helped me from the bottom of his heart. He worked on me for two hours and we spent quite a bit of time talking. I formed friendship ties with Benton's family including his mother Lillian who gave me a warm greeting. Kindness makes the world go round. One trip to Dr. Benton's office saved me years of therapy to come, more medication to fill my blood flow and more support group time. I was cleared spiritually and physically, and the most important thing, I stopped over eating and feeling depressed. I am looking forward to helping Dr. Benton in every way I can.

Clearing this trauma allowed her to trust men again. She was able to find the man of her dreams. A year later, she invited me to her wedding!

Life Changing Experience

The end result of releasing the traumatic memory or memories stored in the emotional aspect of the body is a more neurologically-integrated and healthier person. Clients report that this quick and easy process is pleasant and often life- changing.

As previously mentioned, two ETRT treatments with Joel were sufficient to neutralize his emotional trigger around restaurants, servers, and toothpicks. Joel had suffered a very physical trauma with deep-set emotional ramifications. Often there are traumas that are more invisible, subtle, even translucent—like the graze of a jellyfish's stinger. Traumas typically arise from unexpected situations. Whether mild or severe, the body experiences trauma all at once, both physically and emotionally, in a process which overloads and dims our nervous system. It is inherent in our physiology to react in this manner.

Emotional Traumas have Physical Manifestations

Scientific research has shown that traumas that impact the mind also affect the body. In 1936, the pioneering endocrinologist Hans Selye researched many situations that would impart a traumatic condition—mainly physical stressors. He defined a stressor as a "nonspecific phenomenon representing the intersection of symptoms produced by a wide variety of noxious agents."[16]

Yale University psychologist, John Mason, spent many years measuring hormones in people subjected to various traumatic circumstances. From the 1960s on, new technologies enabled researchers to measure hormone levels, allowing for even greater understanding of stress in the human body. Mason repeatedly challenged Selye to recognize the many flaws in his biological theory and to accept the importance of psychological factors in stress and disease.

In 1972, Johns Hopkins University's clinical scientist Candace Pert discovered opiate receptors in the brain, permitting a new understanding of the relationship between mind and body.[17] These findings led her to a series of groundbreaking conclusions, among them that mind and body are bound together via the neuropeptide communication "messages" through what she calls the "bodymind." She outlined this new view of the body's internal conversation, which appears to be remarkably flexible, varied, and subtle. This was the basis for a new understanding of the connection between emotional and physical trauma.

In the 21st Century, developmental biologist Bruce Lipton, PhD, discusses the distinction between the conscious mind and the subconscious mind. In his YouTube videos _Reprogram your Conscious Mind_ and _Your Body Is An Illusion_ [17.5] he discusses how to reprogram the body-mind. We struggle through life because we are operating from habits we received from other people that we downloaded in the subconscious mind. This occurs in the early formative years. According to Lipton, ninety-five percent of our life is being controlled by these programs, which masquerade as our thoughts. We call them our belief system.

In a revolutionary paradigm shift, Dr. Lipton demonstrated that that what most people conceptualize as our "mind" is, in reality, not located exclusively in our head.

A machine called a Magneto-Encephalograph (MEG) reads brain activity *without* touching a person's head. This technology demonstrates that brain activity is not contained in one's head. Our physical bodies are biochemical, electromagnetic entities that interact and are influenced by all forms of energy. Therefore what we think of as "our mind" is not even physically located in our head! In the quantum, our thoughts are measured as waves.

If we think positive thoughts about someone or something, the person or the scenario tends to connect with us. Conversely, if we think negatively about someone or a situation, this creates a field that resonates with that negative frequency. The concept of bad luck and good luck in relation to our health are merely outward manifestations of our thoughts. We are broadcasting frequencies with our thoughts.

We can change our programs by becoming aware of our subconscious mind and thus re-write the character of our lives. **The Emotional Trauma Release Technique supports our transformation from subconscious programming to conscious choice.** Changing our thoughts changes our manifestation. In this testimonial below you will read how a grandmother's emotional pain appears to manifest as unrelenting lower back pain that abates when the subconscious emotional pain is brought to conscious awareness.

Emotions

Testimonial: Family Trauma

(Alice Sinouhi, Co-Creator with Michael Post of the Samadhi Sea of Wisdom Meditation School, Yuma, AZ)

I met Alice Sinouhi at ServeX Conference in Orange County, CA, in October 2018 where I had just completed my presentation to a large group of entrepreneurs. I taught them that taking care of their body is just as, or even more important than, their prime business, and it should not be neglected in pursuit of worldly gains. And as they work to expand and develop their businesses, they should not overlook the machine that gets them there—their body.

I am in awe and totally love what Dr. Benton has done for me through his almost magical skill of being able to hone in and sense where pain comes from. I had just endured eight grueling hours of excruciating back pain, compounded by the many prior hours of driving to get to the conference.

I have been suffering from back pain for many years, which, if I had to measure, is at a constant pain tolerance level of 10++ with very little relief. Prior to Dr. Benton's treatment, I could not sit for more than 45 minutes at a time without needing to get up and walk around to relieve my back.

As Dr. Benton treated me, he was able to help me see how some "emotional baggage" had become permanently established in my body in the form of pain. When he began exploring the physical areas of pain, I could barely take his touch on my back without screaming and squirming. Needless to say, the pain was intolerable.

Emotional Trauma Release Technique

While muscle testing me and preparing my body for the ETRT release, Dr. Benton asked if I was a mother, a sister, a grandmother. He informed me that he could feel there was a lot of past trauma bottled up inside of me. As he mentioned the word "grandmother," he asked me to touch my forehead. At that moment, I felt something totally releasing from my being, which simultaneously brought up deep emotional pain I have been carrying around concerning my grandchildren. The truth was, my daughter had forbidden me to see my grandchildren, causing me tremendous emotional distress.

This instant release brought all the emotions that had been stored in my body to the surface and forefront of my consciousness. And although I felt the release from my being, I still needed a few more hours to truly process all this trauma I had been carrying around in me for years.

When the healing session was over, Dr. Benton pressed those same areas of my back that had previously been intolerable to touch, and miraculously I no longer felt any pain! After just one session with him, my pain level went down and continues to be at a ZERO!

I live in Yuma, Arizona. Whenever commuting to California, I usually needed to make several stops to alleviate my chronic back pain. I have had back pain for years, and usually needed to make several stops along the way to get out and walk to relieve my back. But after this one treatment by Dr. Benton, I drove straight home from Orange County. I got home at 4:00am. I had so much energy, and best of all did not have to stop along the way!

I highly recommend Dr. Benton for the method he uses for pain relief. More than that, I highly recommend him to be present at events that bring this awareness of healing. I can truly endorse all of Dr. Benton's healing abilities after experiencing first-hand the vibrational impact his technique has on releasing stuck, sub consciousness trauma patterns. The youth counseling work I do with my partner resonates with Dr. Benton's unique Emotional Trauma Release Technique approach. For me it is energy vibration that brings it all together.

Disconnecting from the Emotions

In my experience, people who undergo a traumatic event often find the emotions too overwhelming to deal with. As a survival defense mechanism, they wall themselves off from feeling and being open to any emotion at all. In essence, they become emotionally petrified, by avoiding any and all emotions from being expressed or received. My parents had to do this to survive the Holocaust.

People in this predicament are unaware that it may only take one traumatic experience to activate this complete wall, which shields them from the outside as well as numbs their emotions from the inside. Unlike the gradual buildup of hurt emotion that occurs when we are chronically feeling upset or insecure about a person or a situation, with this wall nothing can come in or out. **If we disconnect from feeling because we have been traumatized in the past, we activate something like a stone wall to protect ourselves. Then, when someone or something new does come into our lives to give us love, we cannot receive it. This "stone wall" we have created to defend ourselves actually blocks us from receiving something good. Our hearts are protected but at the same time**

are also blocked off from our connection to ourselves and others.

This book and ETRT are designed to help you break down the wall and reconnect with yourself by understanding that emotions are not the enemy. Emotions are important feedback and help us to identify where we block and limit ourselves from feeling and experiencing life to the fullest.

What makes the Emotional Trauma Release Technique (ETRT) stand apart from other healing techniques is that it deals primarily with the physiological basis of how these traumatic energies entered our psyche; going back to the root cause, if you will.

Emotions

Notes

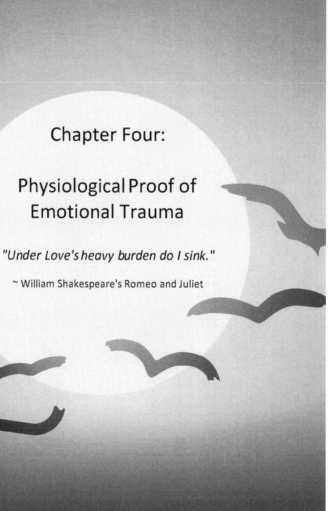

Chapter Four:

Physiological Proof of Emotional Trauma

"Under Love's heavy burden do I sink."

~ William Shakespeare's Romeo and Juliet

ॐ

Broken Heart Syndrome

Who would have believed that broken hearts are not just high school hyperbole? A broken heart is in fact an identified medical condition known as Broken Heart Syndrome.

In 1991, Japanese researchers first recognized Stress Induced Cardiomyopathy or Broken Heart Syndrome, also known as Takotsubo Cardiomyopathy. Although severe and painful, Broken Heart Syndrome is often a temporary condition where the heart muscle is suddenly stunned and so weakened that it assumes a bulging shape resembling an octopus trap, known in Japanese as *tako tsubo*.[18]

Psychological Proof of Emotional Trauma

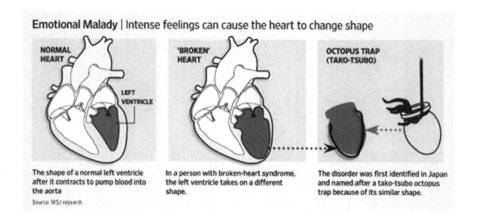

Ron Winslow, Wall Street Journal Article
Hearts Actually Can Break, Feb 9, 2010

This condition is characterized by sudden sharp chest pain and shortness of breath. These symptoms begin just a few minutes to hours after exposure to unexpected stress, which in most cases, are triggered by a tragic event, extreme physical or emotional trauma, such as living through a car accident or experiencing intense grief, anger or surprise at receiving emotionally difficult news.

Researchers think that the stress releases hormones that "stun" the heart and affect its ability to pump blood to the body. The term "stunned" is often used to indicate that the injury to the heart muscle is only temporary. Many seek emergency care, concerned they are having a heart attack.

A study published in the *American Journal of Medicine* in 2015[19] revealed that of their test subjects only ten percent were male, making Broken Heart Syndrome an overwhelmingly female-dominated condition.

Most people who experience Broken Heart Syndrome have normal coronary arteries, without severe blockages or clots. As mentioned previously, the heart cells are "stunned" by stress hormones but not killed. The stunning effects reverse quickly, often within just a few days or weeks. In most cases, there is no lasting damage to the heart.

Yet because these symptoms are similar to a heart attack, it is important to seek help right away. The more fragile a person's health, the more likely their broken heart could worsen their condition. Sometimes, if the pain persists after one to four weeks, patients can receive aggressive treatments such as blood pressure medication and breathing machines.

Researchers from the Minneapolis Heart Institute (MHI) studied two hundred Takotsubo Cardiomyopathy patients' medical histories to identify symptomatic clues to get a better understanding of the innards of a broken heart.[20] "It's not as benign a condition as originally thought," observed Dr. Scott Sharkey, a research cardiologist at the MHI Foundation. "The true mortality rate is only becoming manifest as we have a broader experience with this."

Of the forty-five patients that were treated, nine died despite the interventions administered by medical teams. Sharkey said the study's results were important in highlighting the health dangers of a broken heart, especially for high risk groups such as those with cancer, who were of advanced age, had Alzheimer's disease or suffered from bleeding on the brain.

If you would like to understand this syndrome further, you can reference the *Johns Hopkins Medical FAQ* on Broken Heart Syndrome.[21]

Although it is imperative to always seek medical advice when experiencing something of this nature, I believe that the kinder and more compassionate we are to ourselves and can help to protect us from the extreme effects of Broken Heart Syndrome.

The Brain in Heart[22]

John and Beatrice Lacey were among the first researchers in the field of psychophysiology to examine the interactions between the heart and brain. During the 1960s and 1970s, they observed that the heart communicates with the brain in ways that significantly affect how we perceive and react to the world. Communication along all these pathways also significantly affects the brain's activity. Moreover, messages that the heart sends to the brain also can affect performance.

Prominent physiologist and researcher, Walter Bradford Cannon, hypothesized that when we are stimulated, the mobilizing part—the sympathetic nervous system—energizes us as is indicated by an increase in heart rate. In more quiescent moments, the calming part—the parasympathetic nervous system—calms us down and slows our heart rate. Cannon believed that all of our inner systems are activated together when we are stimulated and calm down together when we are at rest. He proposed that the brain is in control of the entire process.

The Laceys, however, noticed that the model proposed by Cannon only partially matched actual physiological behavior. As their research evolved, they found that **the heart seemed to have its own logic that frequently diverged from the direction of autonomic**

nervous system activity. The heart behaved as though it had a mind of its own.

Additionally, the heart appeared to be sending meaningful messages to the brain, which the brain not only understood but also obeyed. Even more intriguing was the fact that it looked as though these messages could affect a person's perceptions, behavior, and performance. The Laceys identified a neural pathway and mechanism whereby input from the heart to the brain could inhibit or facilitate the brain's electrical activity.

While John and Beatrice Lacey were conducting their research in psychophysiology, a small group of cardiologists joined forces with a group of neurophysiologists and neuroanatomists to explore areas of mutual interest. This represented the beginning of the new discipline now called neuro-cardiology. One of their early findings is that the heart has a complex neural network (communication system) that is sufficiently extensive to be characterized as a "brain in the heart." (Figure 1.2).[23, 24]

The heart-brain, also known as the intrinsic cardiac nervous system, is an intricate network of complex ganglia, neurotransmitters, proteins, and support cells—the same as those of the cranial brain. The heart-brain's neural circuitry enables it to act independently of the cranial brain to learn, remember, make decisions, and even feel and sense.

In terms of heart-brain communication, it is generally well-known that the efferent (descending) pathways from the brain to the heart in the autonomic nervous system are involved in the regulation of the heart. However, it is less appreciated that the majority of fibers in the vagus nerve are afferent (ascending) in nature.

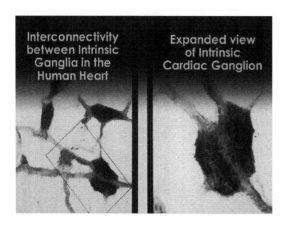

Microscopic image of interconnected intrinsic cardiac ganglia in the human heart. The thin, light-blue structures are multiple axons that connect the ganglia. The image is derived from the work of Dr. J. Andrew Armour MD PhD.

Furthermore, more of these ascending neural pathways are related to the heart and cardiovascular system than to any other organ.[25] **This means the heart sends more information to the brain than the brain sends to the heart.** Recent research shows that the neural interactions between the heart and brain are more complex than previously thought. The intrinsic cardiac nervous system has both short-term and long-term memory functions and can operate independently of central neuronal command.

Case Study: Shoulder Pain and Weakness

A friend and business associate, Nick Delgado, author of *Blood Doesn't Lie*, texted me one morning at 3:02 AM to tell me that the previous evening his left shoulder had gotten weak and sore. He is an avid exerciser, nutritionist, herbal hormone expert, and holds the

Guinness Book of World Records for the most overhead dumbbell presses performed in an hour.[26]

He wanted to know if he needed a hyperbaric oxygen therapy treatment or a chiropractic adjustment or something else. He was concerned because he was scheduled for two speaking engagements the following day, complete with an overhead dumbbell presentation. Obviously, he would not be able to perform any physical activity with a weak and sore left shoulder.

I met him at the Costa Mesa Hilton and waited for other therapists and doctors to perform their various techniques to help him, to no avail. I then asked him if he had experienced anything emotional 24-48 hours prior to the pain presenting itself. He told me that he had indeed heard some heart-breaking news. He had learned that a close friend of his had passed away a couple of days before.

After performing ETRT on him for fifteen minutes, during which time he acknowledged the deep grief he felt for the loss of his friend and shed several tears, he suddenly noticed the left shoulder pain and weakness dissipate. He regained his strength in his shoulder and was able to proceed with his plans under full power. It is noteworthy that the pain he experienced was most likely Broken Heart Syndrome expressing itself in his left shoulder.

Broken Heart Syndrome is not specific to humans. Other creatures experience it as well. An article in the *New York Post* describes the death of a Pomeranian dog named Boo. After the death of his best canine pal, another Pomeranian named Buddy, Boo started developing medical problems. He died soon after, likely of a broken heart.[27]

Notes

Chapter Five:

Genetics vs. Epigenetics

"Genes are the equivalent to blueprints; epigenetics is the contractor."

~ Bruce Lipton, PhD

ಊಊ

Emotional Trauma in the Genes

In 2014, I gave a lecture at the Academy of Comprehensive Integrative Medicine in Dallas, Texas, where I explained to the attendees the difference between genetics and epigenetics, and demonstrated how ETRT neutralizes epigenetic expressions. To explain genetics, I referenced a study by Bachara J. Saab and Isabelle M. Mansuy,[28] who defined inheritance or heritability as the transfer of physical gene characteristics and traits from parents to offspring through genetic processes involving genes and DNA sequences (known as the genome).

Epigenetics, on the other hand, is a process above the genes that involves an ensemble of inheritable changes in gene activity that do not implicate any change in DNA sequencing. Epigenetics refers to external signals that turn gene expression on or off; they affect how cells read genes. This means that a parent's life experiences, in the form of epigenetic tags, can be passed down to future generations. In other words our reactions and predispositions to events and people get passed onto our offspring.

From the point of view of ETRT, epigenetics and trauma concerns our ability or inability to move beyond the combined effect of what we have inherited from our ancestors with our own personal experiences of this lifetime. This also includes the changes in gene expression that will then be passed onto our children.

In Ruth Buczynski PhD's interview in *The Neurobiology of Trauma*, she explains that any person can make a difference in a child's epigenetic development. In that interview, Dr. Dan Siegel confirms that there are four ways we can affect the brain's synaptic connections: synapses, neurons, myelin, and epigenetic controls determine how genes are expressed in the brain. Trauma's impact on epigenetics appear to involve alterations in parts of the genome that would not otherwise be activated. For example, if the genome that is involved in inhibiting inflammation in the body is turned off by epigenetics, inflammation will occur where there is trauma and may remain on after the protective effect of inflammation has passed. This causes chronic inflammatory conditions where no injury can be found.

Epigenetics and Suicide

In 2008, molecular biologist and geneticist Professor Moshe Szyf, PhD and neurobiologist Professor Michael Meaney, PhD examined the human brains of individuals who had committed suicide and compared them with age-related individuals who had died for other reasons. The neural genes in the hippocampus of the suicidal group showed excessive methylation. Methylation is a biochemical process that typically acts to suppress gene transcription (a reaction) from occurring. In suicidal individuals it was found that the area of the brain called the hippocampus—which is associated with converting short term memories into long-term memories—was not as nourished with proteins, as compared with non-suicidal individuals, and did not develop normally.[29]

Researchers at Yale University published a paper[30] correlating early life stress and the inhibition of Ribosomal (RNA) in the developing hippocampus via methylation. It was postulated that suicidal subjects may have been abused as children.

In addition, Professor Meaney hypothesized that certain emotional traits could be passed down through genes inside the brain, and that a parent who experienced a trauma could have certain changes in their brain that might lead to epigenetic changes being passed on, inhabiting the neurons of their children's brains or even their grandchildren's brains. Thus if someone had a parent or grandparent who lived through a genocide, war, witnessing violent death or had suffered a different type of trauma, such as at the hands of an abusive or neglectful parent, that person's offspring would carry traits of the emotional impact in their genes. This works both ways. If, say, a person had loving, nurturing parents, their children and grand-children would receive a positive genetic boost in the psychological and behavioral sense as well.

Professor Szyf also located signs of epigenetic methylation in blood samples. He and other researchers from Yale recruited fourteen Russian children brought up in an orphanage, and compared them with fourteen others raised by their parents. The blood of all the children was analyzed, and it was revealed that the orphans had far more methylation than those who were raised by their parents. Areas of the brain important for communication and brain development were most affected. The study concluded that separation from biological parents causes early stress that affects the person's genome, long-term.

A revelation close to my heart emerged from a study out of New York's Mount Sinai Hospital, where thirty-two Holocaust survivors and their children had their genes analyzed. A methylation tag was found in a stress-related gene in both parents and children alike. "The gene changes in the children could only be attributed to Holocaust exposure in the parents," said Professor Rachel Yehuda, one of the lead researchers on the study. Professor Yehuda also added that other related methylation tags may make us more resilient, which could also be passed down.

Some researchers have taken it a step further, stating that many or even most of our emotional and psychological tendencies—whether we are intellectual or tactile, communicative or quiet, emotional or stoic, forgetful or possess a perfect memory—might arise from epigenetic changes passed down from our ancestors.[31] The evidence suggests that methylation changes the DNA's ability to be expressed.

At the Academy of Comprehensive Integrative Medicine (ACIM) Conference in Dallas, I presented a study on PTSD-afflicted mothers. Children born to these mothers manifested a higher sense of fight or flight instinct. The children of mothers who themselves have a history of childhood physical and emotional abuse have a heightened startle reflex. The children of these abused mothers have greater sympathetic nervous system activation (which responds involuntarily to stressful or dangerous situations) as compared to children of mothers who do not report a history of childhood physical and emotional abuse.[32]

Single Nucleotide Polymorphisms (SNPs)

It is important to understand that the body has the ability to hold onto lifetimes of traumatic events. The study of epigenetics confirms the phenomenon of hereditary trauma being passed on from generation to generation. A modern application of this fact is illustrated in the identification of Single Nucleotide Polymorphisms (SNPs) in the human genome (our DNA). SNPs are defined as a variation in a single base pair in a DNA sequence. This means that over the centuries our base genetic code has changed. In fact, modern science has identified over 1.42 million of these genetic variants.[33] SNPs have taken center stage in genetic testing to identify possible genetic mutations in a person's genome.

An understanding of this phenomena has long been known. The Bible mentions this a few times in the Old Testament. In Numbers 14:18, states: *"The Lord is longsuffering and of great mercy, forgiving iniquity and transgression, and by no means clearing the guilty, visiting the iniquity of the fathers upon the children unto the third and fourth generation."*

Genetics vs. Epigenetics

Personal Case Study

While working toward completing my undergraduate studies at California State Northridge University, I decided to add a minor in chemistry which I completed at Murray State University in Kentucky. As I drove from California to Kentucky, I developed excruciating knee pain in both legs that would vacillate from one to the other. The pain was so intense that I recall hobbling up the stairs to my dorm room like an 80-year-old man. I sought medical treatment with the school nurse, who gave me an option of either consulting a chiropractor or a medical orthopedist. I went to the chiropractor for several visits, which reduced my pain to a manageable level but did not get rid of the problem. I had this knee pain for at least two years.

While studying at the Los Angeles College of Chiropractic in Whittier, California, I had the opportunity to take a class given by Scott Walker, DC, developer of the Neuro-Emotional Technique® (NET). After this class, an associate and I were practicing the technique in clinic. We muscle-tested my body and discovered that there was an emotional trauma stored in my knees. We identified that the origin of this trauma was not mine but in fact stemmed from before I was born. We tracked it back through my father's side of the family, and although it was not my father's personal trauma it originated with the Jewish pogroms of the 12th and 13th centuries. Once I acknowledged this and treated it, the pain miraculously disappeared. While I could not explain the mechanism, I can tell you that this was the first time in two years that my knees were 100 percent pain free!

I am not exactly sure what the trigger was to cause me so much pain. I put it down to the long-distance drive because there had been no physical trauma leading up to it. Through this personal and clinical experience I have learned the following:

- Past traumas from this or other lifetimes can manifest in this lifetime. How many of us have our own tragically ingrained misconceptions of reality, stemming from a great, great, great grandparent to this day?
- Traumas can manifest emotionally, physically or both.
- Holding onto these energies can alter our behavior.
- When the traumatic impact is severe enough, it can cause behavioral changes.
- A great number of genetic variation in our DNA, called Single Nucleotide Polymorphisms (SNP) appear to be due to stress and traumas of the past.
- Getting to the root cause is what neutralizes the impact of the trauma.

Neuro-Emotional Technique® (NET)

As mentioned previously, early in my chiropractic career, I had the opportunity to learn a technique called Neuro-Emotional Technique, developed by Scott Walker, DC. Dr. Walker provided us with a chart indicating where energetic frequencies reside. He revealed that feelings of vulnerability settle in the heart and small intestine meridians. Fear and feelings of paralysis settle in the bladder and kidney meridians. Anger and resentment take hold in the liver and gall bladder meridians, shame resides in the Conception Vessel meridian, whereas grief lodges in the lung meridian.[34]

Epigenetics, Telomeres, and Mindfulness

Recent research tells us that epigenetic changes are often affected by the length of our telomeres. However before I describe the research, it is important to know what telomeres are.

In the NICABM video series, *The Neurobiology of Trauma* interview, Dr. Dan Siegel describes telomeres as follows: "For your cells to stay healthy, your chromosomes (long lengths of DNA) have to unwind and make copies of themselves and then get themselves rewound again. At each end of the chromosomes is a special cap, (like the cap at the end of a shoelace that prevents it from unraveling). Telomeres are the cap on the twisted end of DNA that keeps it intact. They are not genes but the protectors of the genes."

As we age or experience stress, the length of our telomeres shortens. At some point, the number is so low that when the cell divides and puts these two new cells that are made back together, there are not enough telomeres to hold the genetic material together. Once this happens, our cells get sick and die, and we age. Having long telomeres means that we have a lot of these gene-protecting units. Dr. Siegel states that we can repair telomeres with the use of telomerase enzymes, which are activated in part by something called "presence." He says that being aware of what's happening as it is happening is the best predictor of optimal telomerase levels. He believes that presence creates an integrated state of energy and information flow of one's self in one's body and brain and in connection with other people.

Dr. Siegel continues that the brain participates in altering our state of mind. If mindfulness corrects epigenetics, this helps decrease our likelihood of getting inflammatory diseases. This is probably why Felitti found what Felitti found in the ACE study on pages 38-39.

Dr. Siegel believes that dissociation is a curable condition. Our mind can change our molecules. Our presence, thoughts, and mindfulness control the enzyme expression of longevity. With body-mind integration, we can actually optimize telomerase levels and alter epigenetic controls, thus improving cardiovascular function and much more.

Notes

Chapter Six:

Let it Go -
It No Longer Serves You

*Be Content with what you have;
rejoice in the way things are.
When you realize there is nothing lacking,
the whole world belongs to you."*

~ Lao Tzu

☙❧

What is Fear?

British psychologist and educationalist, Charles Wilfred Valentine (1879–1964), wrote the following in his article entitled <u>The Innate Bases of Fear.</u> "The question of the innate bases of fear can hardly be settled except by a careful study of early childhood. To obtain reports from adults about fears that obsessed them, while of great interest and value psychologically in other ways, helps us little as to the problem of innate fears because of the unreliability of the memory of, and indeed the ignorance of, the very earliest experiences which may have started such fears and obsessions. We must turn, then, to the very first months of life, and not merely to study the life of a group of infants at a given period in cross section, as it were, useful as it may be for certain purposes."[35]

But while experiencing fear is stressful to children and parents alike, fear should not be minimized. "A part of normal development, being afraid is a sign that an infant is gaining awareness of the world and trying to make sense of it," says Ari Brown, MD, co-author of *Baby 411* (Windsor Peak Press). Fortunately, most fears arrive at predictable stages, and with some insight, we can help our children navigate their fears and walk more confidently through childhood.

According to research done in 1960, newborns have two fears: loud noises and falling (aka as withdrawal of support).[36] Dr. Brown says, "Babies' brains and nerves grow rapidly in the first two years of life, but they are born with very immature nervous systems, which means that they cannot interpret or handle certain sensory input like loud noises or the feeling of falling." This is why passing an infant around to loving relatives may not bother a baby, but set him or her down too fast or make an abrupt, loud noise, and they will cry in fright.[37]

Lynn Steinberg MFT PhD believes that these two fears—loud noises and falling—are really basic physiological reflexes. She also states that there is another innate psychological fear that is the basis of attachment theory, known as withdrawal of attention. Human and animal babies are born with an instinct to attach to whomever is taking care of them. Ducklings will follow whoever they perceive is the caregiver. This is known as imprinting. Human babies will raise their heads and look in the direction of the voice of the caregiver. Conversely, babies will show signs of fear and agitation when the primary caregiver withdraws attention.

As we grow, we develop more fears associated with culture,

epigenetics, and experiences of our upbringing. Life throws curve balls at us, and whether we duck, catch or get hit, these curve balls often affect us on a conscious and/or subconscious level. When a fear is created from a life experience, the brain generates an emotional marker of this event so as to protect us should something similar arise in the future. Our emotional brain remembers these events for years and is always vigilantly on the lookout for similar scenarios that can cause us to run our defense protocols. This innate defense mechanism is designed to prevent us from re-injuring ourselves.

Over time, this protective system compounds all traumas, fears, and abusive experiences into an amalgamated soup, which expresses itself as stress, anxieties, and phobias. If not addressed (and they rarely are), this soup begins to manifest physically in the body as disease, allergies, auto-immune deficiencies, psychoses, and so on. We may even create alternate realities to cope (see Case Study: Making Lemonade out of Lemons).

This can also result in self-sabotaging habits like Munchausen Syndrome, where the individual needs to stay sick because this is how they have gotten attention in the past. To a lesser degree, people may gain weight as a protective mechanism against being sexually assaulted or attracting a relationship for fear of being emotionally hurt or to protect against verbal abuse, and so on.

We generally forget about these safety mechanisms that have been set in place and now function on auto-pilot. We now have a perpetually running program that says we have to be sick or overweight, or whatever, to be protected. As we get older, we may not even be aware as to why we are always sick or overweight even though we do all the right things to stay healthy.

Now many years later, our emotional brain, which is stuck on auto-pilot in some area(s) of development, does not know that we have grown up. It still utilizes the same defense programs it learned years earlier.

It is important to note that not all auto-pilot programs have their root cause in trauma or fear. They could simply be learned from our parents or environment.

Case Study: Releasing the Past

A male home loan officer in his 30s was experiencing trouble in his work. He was unable to close a couple of deals. With these constant delays and near-misses, he felt his confidence start to erode. Anxiety about his financial well-being, as well as quality of life, began to rise. He writes: "I was involved with three major projects that no matter how much I worked, they were at the edge of failure." He recalls feeling "spiritually dark, full of anxiety. I sensed that I was going through a trial. Dark feelings of failure were engulfing me."

In addition, or even perhaps as a consequence, this man felt physical pain. "I had constant pain in three areas: the left side of my neck, left shoulder, and right in the center of my back." He was not in a good place when he first visited us.

This is what he said after only three sessions of ETRT: "After three sessions with Dr. Benton, the darkness within me was gone and light replaced it. The pain in my back, shoulder, and neck was greatly reduced. I felt that a great problem was in the process of transformation and resolution. It is true that the projects at work did not come to fruition. However, within days, all three projects were transformed, renewed, and were now on the path to completion."

We accept gratitude but we do not look for it or expect it, as our main goal is simply to see people get better. In his letter of deep gratitude toward the staff of the Light Touch Healing Center, he concluded: "Dr. Benton's efforts transformed the darkness to light and the disorganization to order. Dr. Benton truly has a talent and skill to help people resolve their conflicts and resolve their pain."

Let It Go–It No Longer Serves You

Notes

Nurturance or the Lack Thereof

A common theme I have seen with many of my clients is that when they were younger, their parents were not present to their individual needs. Yes, they were provided a home, food, and parental love in the way the parents knew how. However, they lacked the nurturance they desired and this left them limited in their ability to develop a healthy self-esteem and self-worth. Not only did this affect their emotional stance in connection to others, but also their inborn gifts were not encouraged. Such an example might be the child who was born to be a gifted pianist, but could not develop this talent because there was no piano in their home to play, or music lessons provided.

Personally, as a child, I loved to cook. However my mother had other ideas. Even though some of the most famous chefs in the world were men, my mother presumed that cooking was a female skill. Thus my desire to cook was not encouraged, which begs the question: what would have happened had my passion for cooking been nurtured?

Levels of Nurturance

Life skills are one thing. Even more basic is for children to experience physical and emotional aspects of love from their parents. Research validates the notion that babies need to be held, and require hugs for healthy mental and emotional development.

Dr. Gary Chapman's book, *The Five Love Languages*, offers a great discussion of how each of us views nurturance. Dr. Chapman breaks down love into five categories:

Love Language #1: Words of Affirmation
One way to express love is to use emotionally nurturing words that show you understand, appreciate, care for and/or recognize the other person. Verbal sentiments of appreciation are powerful communicators of love. When we receive affirming words we are far more likely to be motivated to reciprocate. If spontaneous compliments mean the world to us, actions do not always speak louder than words. Hearing "I love you," "You look beautiful," "Thank you for taking out the garbage," make us feel appreciated and loved. Conversely, insults can leave us devastated.

Love Language #2: Quality Time
Nothing says "I love you" like full undivided attention. While being there for the other person is critical, REALLY being there—with the TV off, fork down, phone away—makes your significant other feel

truly special and loved. Quality time does not mean that we have to spend our together moments gazing into each other's eyes, even though it could not hurt. It means doing something together and giving our full attention to each other. Distractions, postponed dates, or the failure to listen can be demoralizing.

Love Language #3: Receiving Gifts
This love language should not be mistaken for materialism. If this is our love language, we thrive on gifts of love, especially the thoughtfulness, and effort behind the gift. The perfect gift or gesture shows that we matter, are cared for, and prized above whatever was sacrificed to bring the gift to us. A missed birthday, anniversary or hastily-thought gift can be disastrous as would be the absence of other occasional gestures.

Love Language #4: Acts of Service
Can sweeping the floors or washing the dishes really be an expression of love? Absolutely! Anything you do to ease the burden of responsibility of someone you care about speaks volumes to this type of person. The words they most want to hear are "Let me do that for you." Laziness, broken commitments, and making more work for them tells speakers of this language that they do not matter.

Love Language #5: Physical Touch
For a person whose primary love language is physical touch, hugs, pats on the back, holding hands, and thoughtful touches on the arm, shoulder or face mean the world to them. These gestures translate into "I love you" and "I care about you." Physical presence and accessibility are crucial while neglect or lack of physical contact can be destructive and unforgivable.

Nurturance the Way We Need It

Dr. Chapman says, "If we are to develop an intimate relationship, we need to know each other's desires. If we wish to love each other, we need to know what the other person wants. It is not enough to love someone; more importantly, does this individual feel your love?"

These Five Love Languages are relevant to all of us, whether we are in a love relationship, friendship, work relationship or parent/child relationship, and so on. It is important to be aware of what it takes to have a fulfilling long-term, committed relationship, with less trauma and more nurturance.

In my experience, there is a way of nurturance that enhances these Five Love Languages, known as patience; the ability to give another person the time and space to integrate what you have or are communicating and/or have offered to share. The act of keeping quiet, pausing, and holding space is a powerful tool in the world of relationships.

I learned from Rav Berg of The Kabbalah Centre, a concept known as restriction. Restriction is not repression, it is to pause, while resisting the urge to impose your personal agenda and expectations into the situation. The ability to set positive boundaries or restricting is very empowering.

While understanding these love languages and applying them to open our hearts and nurture our relationships, there may come times, when facing something traumatic, that these positive tools fall by the wayside because the emotions we experience in the moment are so much more intense that they overlay the heart. For example, when a girl I was dating lost her grandmother, our love language was muted by the louder language of sorrow and grief.

The Light of Love

When a flashlight is shone on the wall in a dark room, we can see a clear bright circle of light. If we put a single tissue between the light beam and the wall, the image becomes blurred and dull. Adding several more layers of tissue will almost completely block the transmission of the light.

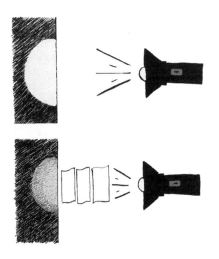

Like the light beam, love shines brightly in an atmosphere of nurturance and acceptance. However, when placed in an environment of rejection or, even worse, in an abusive, traumatic environment, the transmission of love's subtle energy is dimmed like a heart covered in layers of tissue.

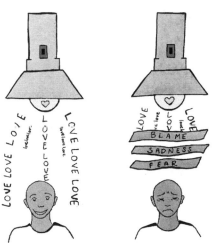

The same is true of the connection between our soul or higher consciousness and God or universal energy. When we behave like God, in other words with the same attributes of sharing, kindness, and mercy, we become close to God. Conversely, when we prefer to be reactive, selfish, and unkind, we not only distance ourselves from God, we also create veils, like the layers of tissues mentioned above, which block the universal energy (Light of God) from flowing to us.

Every interaction has the potential to either build connection or break relationship links not only in our personal lives but also in the world. In his book *Sacred Mirrors: The Visionary Art of Alex Grey*, Alex Grey depicts this energetic connection in his image called Ocean of Love Bliss. He writes: "Relationship gives us access to Divinity through the portal of love. God is love, the attraction that brings beings together.[38]

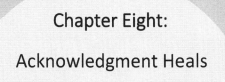

Chapter Eight:

Acknowledgment Heals

"Everything is hard before it is easy."

~ Johann Wolfgang von Goethe

ॐ

Story of Anna O.

In the late 1800s, Josef Breuer and Sigmund Freud recounted the famous case of patient "Anna O."[39]

Ms. O. was 21 years old and had been endowed with a very imaginative mind. She had a strong propensity toward poetry and fantasy. However, she never showed her whimsical, psychic, imaginative, and intellectual life since she was brought up in a puritanically minded family. She had been experiencing a complex array of symptoms including paralysis, convergent strabismus (cross-eyes), and hearing, and eating difficulty. She began to experience hallucinations, deafness then blindness (although her visual faculties were not impaired), and finally paralysis on the left side of her body.

Dr. Breuer writes "No one, perhaps not even the patient herself, knew what was taking place in her. Her condition gradually grew worse ..."

It was discovered that these symptoms were the result of complex emotional trauma experienced as she cared for her ailing father who had fallen ill around July 1880 and succumbed to his illness in April 1881, intertwined with her daydreaming, which she called her "private theater." These symptoms could not be relieved by the simple administration of drugs, or other means.

Joseph Breuer was able to identify the cause of Ms. O.'s trauma through protracted discussions with the patient. Ms. O. was almost lost to reality, trapped in a world of hallucination. Her conversations with Breuer were as if she had spoken to someone in another room. Although her visual faculties were not impaired, she did not see Dr. Breuer in the room with her.

Once this source had been identified, and was "talked through," the symptoms withdrew. In time, Ms. O. came back to the world, healthy, productive, and fully in possession of her senses. "The psychic events of the disease, which produced the sum total of hysterical phenomena, had to be 'talked out,' and with it the symptoms disappeared."

Many of her peculiar and persistent habits disappeared after their causative experiences were related. These experiences, namely the hysterical phenomena disappeared in the hypnosis as soon as she reproduced the events that caused the symptom. "Every single symptom of this complicated, morbid picture was separately taken up backward to the time of its first appearance. When this was related, the symptom was thereby permanently removed. Oftentimes the initial event was related to an interaction with her father, whom she loved passionately."

Dr. Breuer observed that other than her father, Ms. O did not know love. For example, the origin of her becoming deaf was noted by Dr. Breuer as the fear of losing her father each time, and there were 37 instances, where she recalled that he had a chocking attack from swallowing the wrong way. She believed that he would choke himself to death, and since she needed her father so much, she couldn't bear to hear him choking.

Anna O. subjected herself to situations that caused miniature emotional mine-fields to explode. As a result she was drifting away from reality. If it was not for Dr. Breuer and Dr. Freud, she would be another psychotic statistic.

This kind of hypnotic "talk therapy" takes many sessions. And although it works, the Emotional Trauma Release Technique can resolve these types of issues in a more timely manner.

Acknowledgment Heals

Notes

Chapter Nine:

Preparing the Body for the Emotional Trauma Release Techinique™

"Working on nothing less than epic scale."

~ Francis Ford Coppola

෴

ETRT vs Psychology

ETRT is a mind-body technique that addresses a physiological dysfunction, which is an effect of a preceding trauma. ETRT does not cure or heal, it simply neutralizes blocks that prevent the vital energy flow within our body, allowing it to repair and regenerate itself.

Before the discovery of neurotransmitter peptides like serotonin and dopamine, emotions were considered to be largely in the domain of psychology and psychiatry. Now that we know there are molecules that carry emotion throughout the body, any healing art that helps the body neutralize these molecules is beneficial. Today, emotional release techniques are commonplace among acupuncturists,

Preparing the Body for the Emotional Trauma Release Technique

chiropractors, medical doctors, and other healing arts practitioners. ETRT is unique in the world of emotional release techniques because it can be done anywhere, by anyone, and more advanced versions can be performed by ETRT practitioners.

My goal as a practitioner is to help your body be as harmonious and balanced possible. To evaluate your state of well-being, we use a variety of testing methods: physical palpation, range of motion, blood pressure, MRI, blood analysis etc. Applied kinesiology, or muscle testing, is my go-to testing method to evaluate dissonance caused by a traumatic event. Muscle testing is when the practitioner uses resistance of a patient's muscle while palpating areas in their body to find strengths or impairments throughout the body. For example, having the patient hold their arm straight out to their side while the practitioner applies a two finger pressure on the top of the wrist of the extended arm. If the extended arm drops or weakens, this indicates dissonance in the body.

The body is made up of trillions of cells whose proper functioning is regulated by minute electrical impulses. Nerve cells communicate with each other by means of these impulses. To ensure that the body has a necessary level of neurological and muscular integrity for muscle testing to work, a four-part test of communication pathways is applied.

1. Third Eye or Yin Tang Point
2. Hydration Reflex
3. Self-Communication
4. Allergy

When there is harmony along a communication pathway, the specific muscle test will be strong. When there is interference, this is detected by a weakness in a specific muscle. Once this weakness is located, I then search around the body for the point of congruity. I call this process searching for the "short circuit." Oftentimes there are several short circuits that need to be addressed before a muscle test finally stays strong and intercellular communication is restored.

Third Eye or the Yin Tang Point

In the Chinese medicine practices of acupuncture and acupressure, the Yin Tang is the point located between the inner edges of the eyebrows, also known as the Third Eye. It is the energetic expression of the consciousness of the pineal gland. It can be activated via acupuncture, acupressure, or simply by gently guiding one's attention to this area.

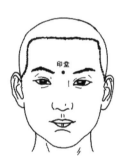

I use this point to connect with the body's inner physician. Touching this point with the pad of index finger switches the energetic polarity, meaning it should make a strong muscle weak and a weak muscle strong. If this does not occur, this indicates a block of this communication system of the body, requiring me to seek and correct the energetic interference.

Hydration Reflex

Hydration is another important element of cellular communication. Our bodies are composed of approximately 70 percent water. Proper hydration is essential to muscular health as well as every process in

Preparing the Body for the Emotional Trauma Release Technique

our body, and is needed to maximize the effectiveness of our healing techniques.

Here are some interesting facts about water and our bodies:

- Our brain is composed of 75% water
- Water makes up 83% of our blood, and carries nutrients and oxygen to our cells
- Water moistens oxygen for breathing
- Water helps convert food to energy and regulates body temperature
- Water removes waste
- Water protects and cushions our vital organs
- Our bones are composed of 22% water
- Our muscles are made up of 75% water

We lose water from our body through perspiration, bowel movements, urine and breath. Before we experience serious signs of dehydration, such as heat stroke, headache, mental fogginess, and fainting, all our muscles will test weak, indicating that you need more water. This reflex is located on both sides of the bridge of the nose.

Self-Communication Reflex

Self-communication is a reflex I learned from Victor Frank DC, developer of Total Body Modification. It involves using the right hand and touching the thymus gland, which is located behind the sternum, with the index finger and the solar plexus with your pinky. If the muscle test weakens while holding this position and testing any strong muscle, this indicates that the body is not communicating with itself and the body energy is fragmented, which needs to be corrected before we can proceed with ETRT.

Allergy Reflex

This reflex point is located at the five o'clock position of the right breast, just outward of the sternum. If the muscle test weakens while holding this position and testing any strong muscle, this indicates that a true allergy or an emotional allergy exists and must be corrected before we can proceed with ETRT.

Preparing the Body for the Emotional Trauma Release Technique

Notes

Chapter Ten:

Emotional Trauma Release Technique™

"I always believe if your are stuck in a hole and maybe things aren't going well you will come out stronger."

~ Roger Federer

൞

The truth of the matter is that truth heals. Imagine being the recipient of a hurtful or snide remark from your co-worker, spouse, child, friend, or lover. Although painful, it is only hurtful to your ego, and is potentially healing for your soul. However as incongruous as it sounds, this is one of the most difficult processes for us to assimilate into actual daily life. Thus what you resist persists. Acknowledging that this remark was hurtful and at the same time understanding that there is a larger lesson to be learned from it, reveals the truth. Congratulations, you have discovered the path to true soul/body healing.

I created the Light Touch Healing Center with the belief that resolving and neutralizing traumatic events reduces stress, makes us younger, and increases our longevity. By combining healing methods, and tailored treatment, we nurture the individual the way *they need it*, and this is when the magic happens.

Emotional Trauma Release Technique™ (ETRT)

ETRT utilizes a combination of thought, breath, and body movement to lessen and relieve blocked energy and uncomfortable sensations associated with traumatic physical and emotional events.

Once the body has been freed of traumatic pain and damage, the mind becomes more receptive. The higher message for this technique is to help bring more trust and more security into interpersonal relationships, and especially the relationship you have with your soul.

ETRT may be beneficial for the following:

Addictions	Urinary Disorders
Anger	Anti-Aging
Anxiety	Auto-Immunity
Abandoned Child Syndrome	Back and Neck Pain
Adverse Childhood Experiences (ACE)	Constipation
	Digestive Disorders
Codependency	Dizziness
Depression	Fatigue
Eating Disorders	Hormonal Imbalance
Emotional Abuse	Irritable Bowel Syndrome
Forgiveness	Joint Aches and Pains
Nervousness	Joint Mobility
Physical Abuse	Knee and Ankle Pain
Post-Traumatic Stress Disorder (PTSD)	Headaches and Migraines
	Muscle Spasms and Aches
Rape	Numbness
Reactive Attachment Disorder	Overweight
Shame	Obesity
Stress	Sciatica
Verbal Abuse	Upper Extremity Pain
Sexual Dysfunction	Highly Sensitive People (HSP)

Unwinding and Down-Regulating the ETRT™ Reflex

When a traumatic event occurs there is a natural reflexive response to step back, look up, and stop breathing called the **ETRT™ Reflex**. This subtle action activates the brain to set a defense marker. The brain takes a snapshot of everything the body is doing in the moment and remembers it. In particular, our posture, the position of our head, the orientation of our eyes, and what we were eating at that exact moment. All these body positions, along with the traumatic event itself, are recorded and memorized in the brain.

With ETRT this process of recording and storing is reversed. ETRT helps to down-regulate the stronghold our emotional memory has on our body's normal physiology by reducing the automatic physiological response to the traumatic event.

Performing the ETRT Process Step by Step

Before I perform ETRT on someone, I first interview the individual to identify the issue. In my practice this interview process happens in two ways. The client may either tells me about an event in their past or I can discover an emotional issue while evaluating a physical symptom they are experiencing, such as pain or a weak muscle response to a test that should normally be strong. Both of these processes activate the emotional memory, which I have found is due to shock trauma almost 90% of the time.

Emotional Trauma Release Technique™ (ETRT)

I ask the client to think about the traumatic event and rate it on an anxiety scale from 1-10, and then to remember that number. I also write the number down. Then, with their eyes open, I ask them to breathe in, extend their neck back and look up, followed by exhaling and looking forward. This process should then be repeated with the eyes closed. The technique is often done while simultaneously tapping the middle of the sternum, which is the heart chakra region.

Once this is complete, I then ask this individual to think about the traumatic event again and rate it from 1-10. This number is often lower. Some of the traumatic memory associated with that particular event has been released. However, there are times when the release of the trauma requires an additional modality. I personally prefer using the Neuro-Emotional Technique® developed by Scott Walker DC (www.Netmindbody.com) in such situations.

When identifying the emotional trauma using muscle testing, I first check all the regular responses to get a base line. I usually use the shoulder muscle. I then ask a client to think of an event. If I get a muscle weakness, I then ask the client to tilt their head back. If the weak muscle now strengthens, this indicates the need for ETRT. I ask the client to keep their eyes open, breath in, gently extend their neck back and look up, then exhale and look forward, while thinking of the event. They then repeat this with their eyes closed. This technique can also be done while tapping their chest in the heart chakra region either by me or by themselves. When the memory of the traumatic event is cleared, this is confirmed by a strengthened response of the arm as they think about the event.

I then have the client close their eyes and think of the same event. If this still results in a weak testing arm, it indicates that the trauma is also in the subconscious. Once again, the client is asked to breathe in and extend their neck back with their eyes closed. The trauma is then partially released from their subconscious. This is confirmed by a strengthened response of the arm in the muscle test.

The reason this technique is so successful is because as I said previously, when one is traumatized, the tendency is to look up and stop breathing, and ETRT unwinds this process. Profoundly simple, this technique brings about dramatic results. The body and mind experience an almost instant release from trauma. I believe that being at peace with anything and everything that life throws our way is vital to living a life of ease and grace.

On page 111 is a form to help you use this technique, which you can also download at http://www.etrt.org

To Summarize, here is the ETRT in steps:

1. Think about the traumatic event
2. What emotion(s) do you experience when thinking about this event (i.e. grief, anger, rage, sadness)
3. Rate the intensity of the emotion(s) on a scale of 1-10
4. Inhale and gently extend your neck backward with your eyes open
5. Exhale and gently flex your neck forward with your eyes open
6. Inhale and gently extend your neck backward with your eyes closed
7. Exhale and gently flex your neck forward with your eyes closed
8. Think about the traumatic event
9. Rate the intensity of the emotion(s) again on a scale of 1-10

Emotional Trauma Release Technique™ (ETRT)

You can repeat steps 1-9 as many times as needed to neutralize all the emotions related to the event. First release the most intense emotion and then work your way through whatever else shows up for you, which may not surface right away but may appear hours or days later.

You can perform ETRT anywhere on your own without any assistance. It can be done with a partner or by someone who knows how to muscle test. Please note that each experience is unique for everyone. Some people feel jovial and more centered after an ETRT session. Yet others could feel more vulnerable and/or teary-eyed. In this instance please take time to breathe deeply, allowing what has transpired to become fully integrated.

Emotional Trauma Release Technique

Emotional Trauma Release Technique™ – worksheet

Think of a painful memory that still haunts you to this day.   Write it below.

Next to it, write a number which best describes the amount of distress that you feel when thinking about this memory.

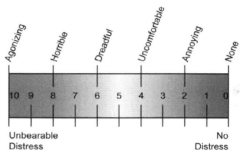

Painful memory #1 _____

_____

What emotion is associated with this memory _____

What distress intensity is associated with the emotion: _____ (initial)

Perform the ETRT as described in my book

After the ETRT procedure:
Think about the painful emotion associated with the memory, and write down a number associated with the distress level.

Distress number: _____ (after)

Jeffrey Benton DC, CTN, QME   **323.297.0566**
© 2014, 2017, 2021

Notes

೫ೕ

Emotional trauma is not limited to the individual. Groups of people can also suffer from pervasive fear that they are subjected to day in and day out, like what happened in Nazi Germany where normal German citizens behaved psychotically towards others in their community. This type of behavior is termed Mass Formation Psychosis.

According to Biomedical Gerontologist Marios Kyriazis,[42] mass psychosis is a psychological epidemic that occurs when a large section of society loses touch with reality and ends up in delusions. Threats (real, imaginary or fabricated) can turn a society of weak and vulnerable people into a state of mass psychosis. Those who suffer from this condition do not realize that it is happening, and subconsciously sink into a lower moral and spiritual level, causing them not only to suffer trauma and fear but it also affects their emotional stability, making them more irrational, irresponsible, unstable, and unreliable, and worst of all, possibly do things so against their nature like commit bad deeds they would otherwise never commit.

He says that to escape from this situation the individual tries to reclassify his inner world with a situation that combines real events and fiction, to put an end to the feeling of panic. This perception is abnormal, based on illusions and not on positive ways of adjusting. It allows the person to escape from these negative emotions but at the cost of losing touch with reality.

Dr. Robert Malone MD, MS[43] states that most of what he has learned about mass formations psychosis theory has come from Dr. Mattias Desmet, a psychologist and a statistician at the University of Ghent in Belgium, who realized that this form of mass hypnosis—the madness of crowds—can account for the strange phenomenon of about 20-30% of the population in the western world becoming entranced with the Noble Lies and dominant narrative propagated and enforced by politicians, science bureaucrats, pharmaceutical companies, and legacy media.

He explains that those hypnotized by this process are unable to recognize the lies and misrepresentations they are being bombarded with on a daily basis, and actively attack anyone who has the temerity to share information with them that contradicts the propaganda they have come to embrace. And for those whose families and social networks have been torn apart by this process—and who find that close relatives and friends have ghosted them because they question the officially endorsed "truth" and are actually following the scientific literature—this can be a source of deep anguish, sorrow, and psychological pain.

The conditions to set up mass formation psychosis include lack of social connectedness and sense-making as well as large amounts of latent anxiety and passive aggression. When people are inundated with a narrative that presents a plausible "object of anxiety" and strategy for coping with it, then many individuals group together to battle the object with a collective singlemindedness. This allows people to stop focusing on their own problems, avoiding personal mental anguish, and instead focus all their thought and energy on this new object.

As mass formation progresses, the group becomes increasingly bonded and connected. Their field of attention is narrowed and they become unable to consider alternative points of view. Leaders of the movement are revered, unable to do no wrong.

Dr. Malone explains that left unabated, a society under the spell of mass formation will support a totalitarian governance structure capable of otherwise unthinkable atrocities to maintain compliance. Even when the narrative falls apart, the hypnotized crowd cannot break free of the narrative. Those being controlled by mass formation no longer are able to use reason to break free of the group narrative.

The obvious example of mass formation is Germany in the 1930s and 40s. How could the German people, who were highly educated, very liberal in the classic sense; western thinking people, go so crazy and do what they did to their fellow man?

Mass Formation Psychosis and ETRT

Dr. Malone explains that a leader of a mass formation movement will use the platform to continue to pump the group with new information to focus on, and uses the term "fear porn." Leaders, through main stream media and government channels continuously feed the "beast" with more messaging that focus and further hypnotize their adherents.

I have found that ETRT can help liberate a person caught in this illusionary fear cycle from their psychotic responses to their environment around them. My hope is that as more people become less fearful, more mindful, and use common sense they will reconnect to their own truth, re-awaken their internal power and realize that the universe supports them, which will have a quantum positive cosmic effect on others in the world at large.

Chapter Twelve:

My Mission-
A Joyous and Harmonious Life

"Who is Rich? One who is satisfied with his lot."

~Ethics of the Fathers, Chapter 4:1

Chiropractic

Dr. Edward Wagner DC explains that the lack of communication between systems in the body is the cause of all disease.

I would not have developed the Emotional Trauma Release Technique had I not gone through the training and licensure of the healing arts known as chiropractic and applied kinesiology.

The common view is that chiropractic is merely the manipulation of joints and soft tissues, yet it is so much more than that. Chiropractic manipulation removes blockages from the nervous system, allowing the body, mind, and spirit to realign physically, emotionally, and spiritually. It up regulates the parasympathetic nervous system (resting response), down regulates the sympathetic nervous system (fight, flight or freeze), and re-establishes enhanced communication between bodily systems. What looks like a simple adjustment of the spine actually can do any or all of the following:

- Stimulate the immune response
- Reregulate the digestive, circulatory, neuro-musculo-skeletal, endocrine, reproductive, and lymphatic systems.
- Bring the body to poise (balance).
- Energize the spirit.
- Create a sense of peace and harmony within.

Chiropractic is the gateway to vitalism. The Merriam-Webster Dictionary defines vitalism as: *1: a doctrine that the functions of a living organism are due to a vital principle distinct from physiochemical forces; and 2: a doctrine that the processes of life are not explicable by the laws of physics and chemistry alone and that life is in some part self-determining.*

In 2011, nine researchers, using a Positron Emission Tomography (PET) scanner, measured changes in twelve male volunteers after each received one Chiropractic Spinal Manipulation (CSM).[40] A brain PET scan was performed twice on each participant, once at rest prior to the treatment and then again after CSM. Comparisons of questionnaires indicated a lower stress level and better quality of life after the treatment.

The researchers discovered that:

- Cervical muscle tone decreased, having an anti-stress effect on the muscles in the neck

- Salivary amylase decreased, indicating a drop in the feeling of being stressed
- Regional brain metabolic changes occurred in different areas of the brain, thus confirming that the brain is greatly influenced by a spinal adjustment

This study confirmed how effective chiropractic spinal manipulation is to brain function and thus the central nervous system.

In short, we humans are more than the sum of our physical parts. Our bodies possess an organic-electromagnetic harmony, which I describe as our Life-Force energy, also known as chi (qi). Every sub-atomic particle of every atom of every cell contains this force. This phenomenon is confirmed in the works of Dr. David Hawkins: *Power vs. Force: The Hidden Determinants of Human Behavior*; Andrew Weil M.D.: *The Natural Mind*; Dr. Deepak Chopra: *The Healing Self*; Rav Berg: *To the Power of One* and *Miracles, Mysteries, and Prayer*, and many others.

In recent years, the medical community has steered patients towards chiropractic, osteopathic, physical therapy, acupuncture, and other such physiotherapeutic practices. Chiropractic is one of the largest complementary medical practices in the United States, having experienced an industry growth of more than 35% since 1990.

As someone steeped in the healing arts, my mission is to bring greater awareness to all of humanity about how to attain a joyous and harmonious life through self-care and healing. In my opinion, most of us settle for mediocrity, which takes on the form of living the symptom-free existence of: take the pill, get the injection to make the pain go away.

My Mission: A Joyous and Harmonious Life

I feel a responsibility to re-educate others in defining what it is to be alive. Being alive is different from existing day-to-day, while dealing with all kinds of aches, pains, and problems—both physical and emotional. Being alive is living in alignment with our purpose. As we grow toward living our purpose, it becomes easier to let go of the circumstances and fears we allowed to enslave our power. We become filled with vitality, youthfulness, joy, and gratitude.

The ETRT allows you to be vulnerable and feel safe enough to acknowledge your shame and the other emotions that hold you back from truly being all powerful, recognizing your self-worth, and living an amazingly brilliant life.

True Health

What is true health? From my experience, true health exists in the plane of experiential bliss, which is beyond the reality of good and bad, ups and downs, right and wrong. It is a plane where we experience boundless freedom, limitless Life-Force energy with no fragmentation, and no separation from source. Fragmentation creates discord, whether it is in the body or spirit, resulting in disharmony in our bodies as well as in our relationships with ourselves and others.

Achieving optimal health is not only about taking tons of supplements; nor is it about the latest health craze. We are designed perfectly in God's image. Why mess with a good thing? Our innate bodily systems do not need to be told what to do, what to take, what and when to eat, and with what to be injected. These systems function without our input, and that is awesome. We truly need to appreciate the perfection that is us.

Our greatest downfall is the ego, which in reality is not part of who we are (but that is for another book). The ego is all about pride, anger, doubt, entitlement, hatred, shame, and judgment of ourselves and others.

In his book *On World Peace: Two Essays by the Holy Kabbalist Rav Yehuda Ashlag*[41] Rav Ashlag (1885–1954), known for his Hebrew translation and commentary of the ancient Aramaic text of the Zohar, explains:

It is widely known that during the days of Creation, the Creator did not complete His Creation. This is why we find that each and every part of reality, both in general and in its particulars, is subject to the laws of gradual evolution, from a state of complete absence all the way to the point of its maximum growth.

This is the reason why, for example, when we taste the bitterness of a fruit in its initial stages of growth, we do not judge this to be a [lit. as an existence of] fault or blemish in the fruit. We all know the reason for the bitter taste: It is because the fruit has not yet completed its [growth or] process of evolution all the way to the ultimate end.

This, too, is the case with all other particular parts of reality. Thus, if we feel that some particular part of Creation is destructive or evil, this indicates only that it is in a transition phase in terms of its evolutional process. In any case, we should not conclude that it is not good and find faults in this particular part, for this would be unwise.

As very young children, most of us lived free and with hardly a care in the world. We scampered about, hatched plans and stratagems.

We took each day as a matter of course. We were mischievous, got angry, got happy, forgave and forgot, and lived life with a sense of wonder. Could we, just possibly, live that way again?

Unfortunately, as we grow, we are trained to not check in with our heart and tend to lose our spiritual footing. We are taught to limit our potential with rules and regulations, and that material things are what create happiness. This is described by Bruce Lipton, Ph. D in his book *Biology of Belief*, where he explains how our personal beliefs affect our biology. As a result, our spirit and Life-Force connection dims. We get so used to the burden of accumulated stress that we no longer remember our earlier joys, which have been trained out of us by our parents, teachers, culture, and environment.

As we age, our happiness becomes defined by our culture, which is heavily marketed to us by large corporations wanting us to purchase their goods and services as our next "dose of happiness." But that still is not enough. Our desire is insatiable. The hunger never ends.

People who are freed from trauma, although escaping its hold, do not forget these distressing events entirely, of course. It is not amnesia we are providing. However, these traumatic events no longer need to weigh heavily upon them as they once did. These past traumas can be reflected upon with a sense of tranquility.

ETRT is a bridge to assist you in taking small steps toward your revitalization. The first step is to allow yourself to be vulnerable, to courageously access those old traumas stored away in your subconscious. The second step is to use this breathing and heart tapping technique to neutralize some of the effects of these traumas.

Use ETRT to release some past shame, guilt, and/or pain to the point where you feel more comfortable being vulnerable and courageous to be you. This is the birth place of joy and love.

People who are happy, who feel purposeful and full of vitality, do not crave physical possessions in the extreme or linger upon their times of pain and misfortune. They cast off the gloom and learn to live life anew. They move forward to productive and pleasurable activities.

A leading researcher in the field of human connection, Brené Brown PhD, lectures worldwide about connection, disconnection, and shame. While speaking at a Ted Talk in 2010, she openly shared her own failings and limitations of being human. By doing so, she was being courageous by allowing herself to be vulnerable, which she explained "allowed us to 'see' her." Ms. Brown notes that for connection to happen, we have to allow ourselves to be vulnerable. In her 2013 Ted Talk, she clarified her definition: "Being vulnerable is our most accurate measurement of courage. Vulnerability is the birthplace of innovation, creativity and change."

Ms. Brown distinguishes the winners from the quitters as those people who have love and belonging, and have an internal belief that they are worthy of love and connection.

It is wonderful to witness the transformation of clients while they experience ETRT, neutralizing and releasing the anchors of past trauma. Their demeanor seems to change instantly, leaving them feeling like a weight has lifted off of them.

ETRT is a simple technique to uplift your life. It is natural, safe, and non-invasive. I am happy to share this technique with you. I cannot

My Mission: A Joyous and Harmonious Life

wait to hear your stories of healing successes. For more advanced trauma release and other cutting edge healing methods, feel free to contact our Los Angeles office.

Jeffrey Benton DC CTN, ACN, QME
(323) 297-0566
www.ETRT.org
FB: https://www.facebook.com/jeffrey.d.benton
IG: https://www.instagram.com/lthcenter/
LinkedIn: https://www.linkedin.com/in/drjeffreybenton

ಎఈ

Breaking the Negative Cycle

Irene V. came to me bewildered, asking for my help. She was sure in her heart that she was done with her traveling salesman boyfriend. She could not understand why, when she heard his voicemail on her answering machine, she had to return his call, which would inevitably lead to them getting together again. This pattern of behavior occurred several times, and she wanted out. After an ETRI session, Irene discovered that as a child, her mother had taught her that it was impolite to not return phone calls. This epiphany cleared her auto-pilot program to always return a phone call, no matter what. She no longer felt the need to ever return his call again.

Additional Case Studies

Making Lemonade Out of Lemons

Early in my career I treated a retired actress, who was practically a real-life Cinderella. While she was still very young, her mother passed away and her father re-married. She inherited a harsh stepmother, and cruel stepsisters. She felt ostracized and abandoned. To survive, she withdrew and created an alternate fantasy world for herself, complete with characters whom she would portray.

Adapting to her bleak and hostile surroundings was the catalyst to her creating a successful acting career. When she was older, she became an actress and played numerous theatrical roles. Although she had gained fame and fortune, she came to see me because she felt disconnected from her essence. After a few sessions of ETRT, it became clear that, although she had successfully adapted, in order to survive and turn out to be a successful member of society, parts of her emotional and spiritual growth were impeded. She was never nurtured the way she craved. She realized that this is what led to her not being connected to her essence. By releasing her feelings around nurturing or lack thereof, she was able to feel connected again.

Accidental Fall

A young woman came to see me after accidentally tripping and landing heavily on the pavement. She walked into the office, bent over, stiff with pain to her upper body, neck, and hips. I asked her to lie down and began testing and rebalancing her bruised and sore muscles. I asked her to recall the accident as I worked with different parts of her body. Her emotional attachment to the unexpected fall and the subsequent trauma of the incident were instantly released.

The entire consultation lasted a whole ten minutes!

She left our office walking straight up, not bent over, in less pain, and smiling.

Sleepless Nights

I have a client who was never able to get restful sleep. She was caught in a Catch-22 conundrum that started when she was a little girl. Upon questioning, we were able to uncover that she was afraid to go to sleep as an adult due to bad dreams.

As a child, she had scary dreams that would awaken her and she would run to her parents' room. The door was always shut and she was not allowed to enter. She recalls falling asleep on the floor outside their door, as she was too afraid to go back to her bed alone. And to make matters worse, when her parents found her asleep at their bedroom door, she was admonished for falling asleep outside their door instead of comforted and nurtured.

As a result she did not like to fall asleep at all at night. Her parents grew infuriated with her for staying awake. Yet although she was scared to fall asleep, she still wanted to be good in her parents' eyes. Her parents would not even support her when she had a bad dream. Lying in bed at night was torture because she was afraid to fall asleep and also afraid to stay awake.

After her ETRT, she was able to get a night of restful sleep. Treatment is continuing.

Additional Case Studies

Notes

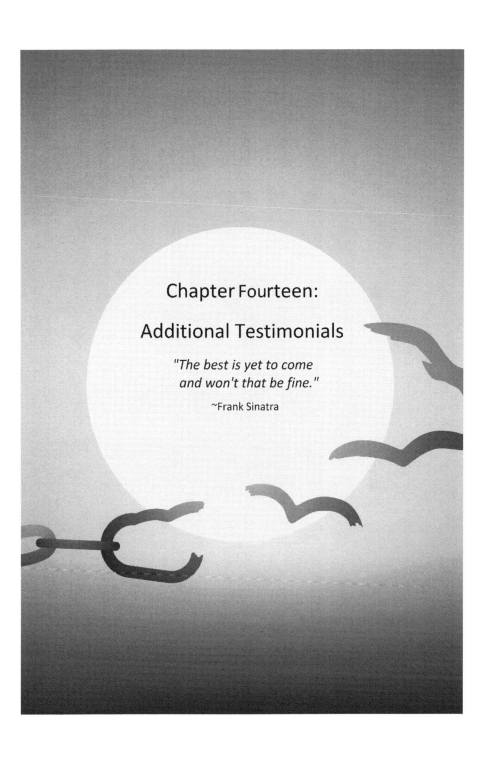

❦

Wow. I cannot believe healing can happen so fast. I was four days into feeling crappy. I was coughing, stuffy nose, feverish and worst of all was I had no voice. I coach women to find the root cause of their excess weight, so they can release it and look and feel amazing. So for my business, not to mention my personal life, my voice is everything. And I had no voice.

I signed up for a networking meeting and had laryngitis, leaving me with no voice. I arrived at the event with two pads of paper and a pen, ready to meet new people, but without being able to speak. I could just barely strain to get a whisper at best.

Dr. Jeffrey Benton arrived at the event and greeted me, hearing (or not) that I had no voice. He asked if I'd like to get my voice back and I agreed vigorously. He suspected there was an unresolved emotional issue.

Addfitional Testimonials

We stood on the sidewalk, outside the restaurant where the networking group was. Dr. Benton started asking my body questions. It must have looked pretty odd to be standing on the street with my left arm in the air, and the doc pushing down on it. The strength of my arm weakened as certain questions were asked, telling Dr. Benton which path of inquiry to follow.

Within 10 minutes, we had an answer— my voice was missing because of a situation in my personal life where I felt I had no voice. A couple more questions, standing there on the sidewalk, and my voice was back!! I could talk! Within minutes I had my voice back after three days of silence. And that's not nearly as good as what Dr. Benton can do in his Light Touch office. This was on the sidewalk outside Jimmy's Famous American Tavern.
~Alaina S.

༄༅།

I'm amazed at what Dr. Benton does. I met Dr. Benton at our Chanukah Party, hosted at Busby's. As the event was winding down, he was kind enough to offer to buy my husband a beer, and offered to buy me one as well. I was on Sudafed for what I thought was a sinus infection for over three weeks, and declined the invitation. We got to talking and when he became aware of my health predicament, Dr. Benton offered to work on me right there in the room. Ever since I returned from Israel four weeks ago, I've been struggling. I even went to urgent care and they wanted to give me a steroid injection. No thank you.

Dr. Benton asked me to raise my arm, and did some muscle test. I don't know what he did, but he cleared something out of me right there! I never knew healing could happen that way. He told me that my immune glands were weak and that he would need to perform a nutrition evaluation on me to find out exactly what I needed. He assured me that I would not need to take any conventional medication, only natural vitamins, herbs and homeopathic remedies.

The next morning I went to his office. He performed a full session and uncovered weak reflexes. His insights were spot on. Everything about what he did blew me away.
~Rebbetzin Esther S.

"I was very privileged to work with Dr. Benton. I had a lot of emotional trauma around relationships. In two sessions my trauma was reduced by 60 percent. Dr. Benton has the gift of finding what the root cause is and removing it.

As a 4th generation intuitive healer myself, I recognized the huge gift of healing that Dr. Benton has. Every time I have emotional challenges I come to Dr. Benton. I can't recommend him enough."
~Veronica R.

"Dr. Benton is a miracle worker. He not only was able to heal my shoulder that was terribly dislocated from softball in SECONDS, but was able to heal my rotator cuff. This ongoing pain had been occurring for five years, and in just a minute, he healed it all. We have

Addfitional Testimonials

now been in contact discussing his works with trauma patients dealing with PTSD, and chiropractic works."
~Gina M.

"I had been suffering from severe low energy for eight years. Anxiety and panic attacks due to emotional and physical abuse as a child. After only one session with Dr. Benton, I felt an increase in energy, much less anxiety, and renewed feeling of calm. After seeing numerous doctors with little or no benefit, Dr. Benton just in one session helped dramatically!"
~H. D., Central Los Angeles

I was prescribed Pantoprazole, one per day, Ondansetron in case I began vomiting, and Tramadol for pain, is the best my M.D. could do for me. Then I was referred to Dr. Benton by one of my dearest friends, who told me that he was an excellent physician (chiropractor) and was serious about treating his clients emotionally through an amazing technique called ETRT.

I had developed acute gastritis, which in general terms means an inflammation of the stomach lining. I am knowledgeable in the benefits of nutrition, organ deregulation, naturopathic as well as homeopathic visceral organ release, and osteo-mobilization methods to change conditions in the human body, yet I could not seem to recover from this very painful condition.

The most important key was that I could not treat myself. In my opinion, no human being can treat themselves. I told Dr. Benton that I was in pain and had done everything I knew how to heal my illness. Dr. Benton replied: "Let's see what we can do." I completely trusted my care to Dr. Benton to use all of his knowledge to help me. He tested me to check for organ dysregulation. He administered key nutritional supplements that were specific to both my emotional trauma and the organ systems affected, and within eight hours my symptoms had completely disappeared. He worked on me to help me release the fear and anxiety I had internalized from a prior terrible experience.

I am so thankful that there is a truly great physician (chiropractor). He is an Angel of God who has changed my life. My faith in Integrative Medicine has been fortified through Dr. Benton's knowledge, professionalism, and treatment method. If you truly want to be healed I want to introduce you to Dr. Jeffrey Benton and the Light Touch Healing Center.
~Bethany B., Los Angeles

"I recently went into the Light Touch Healing Center, where I was treated by Dr. Benton. It was a great experience. I was suffering from concussion symptoms after a recent traffic accident. I felt neck pain and was having trouble lying down with any comfort while sleeping. Dr. Benton relieved these symptoms. After my session, my neck was not painful. I got a great night's sleep. Also, I was not feeling groggy, which I understand is a concussion symptom. I definitely recommend Dr. Benton and his courteous and professional staff. I've already

recommended them to friends. I just didn't want to be weighed down by this stuff, and now I feel clear and functional again."
~James C., San Francisco

꙳

"Dr. Jeffrey Benton performed his technique Emotional Trauma Release Therapy and all I can say is I was a new woman walking out of his office. I felt that all the blockages holding me back in life were finally released. Thank you Dr. B."
~Kimberly B., Studio City

꙳

"Dr. Jeffrey Benton definitely has a light touch, which is so rare in today's therapeutic industry. Bedside manner is virtually non-existent. However, Dr. Benton is gentle, caring, and great at listening to you and your body. He helped me quickly pinpoint an emotional trauma that I was holding in my body from 20 years ago, during one visit. He then proceeded to isolate [the trauma] and guided me to release it. It's been a week and still no pain on that once very sore and locked-up side of my body. His ETRT worked wonders for me."
~Djakarta A., Los Angeles

꙳

"Don't think twice. Dr. Benton is the real deal! He is absolutely amazing. There were a few situations when he helped me! I will just

share two for now. I had an interview scheduled with a major TV network, to be an assistant editor for a TV show. He picked up on the fact that I was not only very nervous but that there was a certain amount of doubt that I needed to overcome if I really wanted the position. The interview was the next day; Dr. Benton worked on me and I got the job! The second time, I was getting headaches. He worked on me and it helped me a LOT!"
~Tang T., Santa Clarita

I first met Dr. Benton because I was involved in a car accident. I needed a doctor who is open late because I just started a new job and could not miss any work. My attorney referred me to Dr. Benton. This is my story:

When I was 17 years old (and I am 49 now) I was choked by an assailant, and as he grabbed me on my neck, his thumb dug into the left side. Ever since then, my neck has always hurt on the left side. I thought I would have to live with this pain forever, but that was not true. I realized that pain can be relieved with the right care. Although this pain had always bothered me, it is almost gone now. This is the result of the care I received from Dr. Benton. I have less pain now than I ever had since the attack.

When I was 21 years old, I was in the army and I fell down a 750 foot cliff, before grabbing onto a tree. I hit my upper back under my shoulder blades on one tree and my lower back and hip on another tree. I had been in pain ever since. However, when I went to see Dr. Benton he was able to take all my pain away. This was the first time

Addfitional Testimonials

I had been pain-free in 20 years!

Anyone in pain should not give up. Go find your solution. It's amazing how far treatment can go. I am living proof of that treatment. Even after many years, it is possible. Get rid of your pain and make yourself a better life. Take good care of yourself. You deserve the best and nothing less.

~Cherie Salinas

I hope this book helps you transform your life with Light and Love.

I pray that you live a life of love, acceptance, and forgiveness with an attitude of gratitude.

~ Jeffrey Benton, DC CTN ACN QME

ABOUT THE AUTHOR

Dr. Jeffrey Benton is a licensed chiropractic healer who has spent much of his life studying the human body. He received his doctorate in Chiropractic in 1996 from the Southern California University of Health Sciences and has been a Certified Traditional Naturopath since 2010. In 2014, Dr. Benton became a qualified medical examiner for the State of California, and in 2016 he received certification in Applied Clinical Nutrition.

Dr. Benton has been featured on CBS Evening News, and lectures nationwide. He has presented at the Five Dimensions of Life event in Los Angeles, the Pathways For Vets symposium in Colorado, White Memorial TMJ Pain Clinic in Los Angeles, Bio-ReGenesis Anti-Aging Conference in La Costa, the Academy of Comprehensive Integrative Medicine in Dallas, as well as the Academy of Integrative Health and Medicine in San Diego. Dr. Benton is the recipient of the Amare "I Am Enough Movement™ Heroes of Change" award in 2021. He received the EZ Way Health Professional of the Year Award for the year 2019 and was named Top Chiropractor in Los Angeles Magazine for 2018 and 2019.

Dr. Benton uses light touch, humor, empathy, and specific chiropractic techniques to help the body reboot. This protocol improves the body's internal self-correcting program, thereby

About the Author

reconnecting you to health and vitality. He focuses on helping to reset all the major areas of neuro-musculo-skeletal dysfunction.

Besides his busy private practice, Dr. Benton also travels extensively throughout the world consulting with people and businesses and to help them build a stable platform for health and vitality. Dr. Benton lives in Los Angeles.

www.ETRT.org

FROM THE PUBLISHER

In my career I have helped thousands of authors develop and write their books to share with humanity. Every so often, a book appears on my desk that stands out, and is revolutionary. The _Emotional Trauma Release Technique™: The Ultimate System for Releasing Life Traumas_ is one such book. In this user-friendly how-to guide, Dr. Jeffrey Benton has uncovered the mysteries of releasing trauma.

In the genre of health and wellness, I believe that this book is the proper successor to _The Secret_ by Rhonda Bryne because our biggest obstacles are what we believe subconsciously. As you will have read, these limiting and destructive beliefs often come from traumas we endured in childhood. It is no wonder that when reading the first few chapters you learn that this technology was developed from a broken heart.

In this inspirational book, Dr. Benton illustrates how releasing the remnants of past traumas lingering in your soul can result in a state of wholeness, empowerment, joy, and fulfillment.

~ Raymond Aaron

ENDNOTES

Introduction:
[i] https://www.cdc.gov/mmwr/volumes/71/su/su7103a1.htm?s_cid=su7103a1_w
[ii] https://www.cdc.gov/nchhstp/newsroom/docs/factsheets/dash-mental-health.pdf

Chapter One:
[1] Cannon W.B. *The importance of Emotional Attitudes for Good Digestion.* Dept. Physiol. Harvard Med Sch. Journal of the American Dietetic Association 1939 Vol 15. Pp 333-344
[2] Piper DW, Greif M, Shinners J, Thomas J, Crawford J. *Chronic Gastric Ulcer and Stress. A Comparison of an Ulcer Population with a Control Population Regarding Stressful Events over a Lifetime.* Digestion 1978; 18 (5-6); 303-9
[3] Veenstra RP etal. *Acute Stress-Related Gastrointestinal Ischemia.* Digestion 2007 75 (4): 205-7. Epub 2007 Oct 5

Chapter Two:
[4] https://today.uconn.edu/2016/02/brain-imaging-technology-reveals-hidden-emotions/
[5] http://emotionresearcher.com/the-emotional-brain/panksepp/
[6] Quirk GJ, Beer JS. *Prefrontal Involvement in the Regulation of Emotion: Convergence of Rat and Human Studies.* Current Opinion Neurobiology. 2006 Dec16 (6):723-7
[7] Dr. Sebern Fisher. *Neurofeedback in the Treatment of Developmental Trauma: Calming the Fear Driven Brain.* W. W. Norton & Co, Inc., 2014

Endnotes

Chapter Three:

[8] https://www.ted.com/talks/lisa_feldman_barrett_you_aren_t_at_the_mercy_of_your_emotions_your_brain_creates_them

[9] Caroline Markolin PhD. *German New Medicine ® (GNM)* EXPLORE! Magazine, Vol. 16/Nr. 2 - 2007

[10] Susan Silberstein PhD. *Dr. Ryke Geerd Hamer Creator of the New German Medicine* © Beatcancer.org

[11] David R. Hawkins. *Power Vs. Force: The Hidden Determinants of Human Behavior.* Hay House Inc., 1994, p.68-69

[12] Vincent J Felitti, MD. *The Relation between Adverse Childhood Experiences and Adult Health: Turning Gold into Lead.* Perm J. 2002 Winter; 6(1): 44–47.PMCID: PMC6220625 PMID: 30313011

[13] https://www.huffpost.com/entry/the-adverse-childhood-exp_b_1943647

[14] *The Adverse Childhood Experiences Study — the Largest Public Health Study You Never Heard Of* 10/08/2012 09:02 am ET Updated Dec 06, 2017

[15] *The Adverse Childhood Experiences (ACE) Study.* CDC .gov. Atlanta, Georgia: Centers for Disease Control and Prevention, National Center for Injury Prevention and Control, Division of Violence Prevention. May 2014. Archived from the original on 27 December 2015.

[16] Hermona Soreq, Alon Friedman, Daniela Kaufer. *Stress—From Molecules to Behavior: A Comprehensive Analysis of the Neurobiology of Stress Responses.* Wiley, 2010

[16.5] Selye H, *The Stress of Life*, McGraw-Hill, USA, c 1956

[17] Candace Pert. *Molecules of Emotion: The Science Behind Mind Body Medicine.* Touchstone, 1999

[17.5] Bruce Lipton Ph.D. Your Body Is An Illusion https://youtu.be/AjLGg9qgfWo, How to Reprogram Your Subconscious Mind https://youtu.be/OqLT_CNTNYA

Chapter Four:

[18] https://weblog.wur.eu/international-students/2018/02/23/ive-been-diagnose-of-bhs-broken-heart-syndrome/

[19] Pelliccia F, Kaski JC, Parodi G, Greco C, Antoniucci D, and Brenner R, et al. *Comorbidities Frequency in Takotsubo Syndrome: An International Collaborative Systematic Review Including 1,109 Patients.* American Journal of Medicine. 2015

[20] http://www.medicaldaily.com/broken-hearts-can-be-matter-life-and-death-real-dangers-heartbreak-325888

[21] www.hopkins medicine.org/asc/faqs.html

[22] https://www.heartmath.org/research/science-of-the-heart/heart-brain-communication/

[23] Armour, J.A. *Anatomy and function of the intrathoracic neurons regulating the mammalian heart, in Reflex Control of the Circulation,* I.H. Zucker and J.p. Gilmore, Editors. 1991, CRC Press: Boca Raton. p. 1-37.

[24] Armour, J.A., *Potential clinical relevance of the 'little brain' on the mammalian heart.* Exp Physiol, 2008. 93(2): p. 165-76.

[25] Cameron, O.G. *Visceral Sensory Neuroscience: Interception.* 2002, New York: Oxford University Press.

[26] https://www.youtube.com/watch?v=MgpzOMQ-wPo

[27] https://nypost.com/2019/01/19/worlds-cutest-dog-boo-dies-from-a-broken-heart-owners/

Chapter Five:

[28] Bechara J. Saab and Isabelle M. Mansuy January 1, 2014 J Exp Biol 217, 94-101. doi: 10.1242/jeb.089995 Wikipedia definition of Brca1 Brca2

[29] Patrick O. McGowan, Aya Sasaki, Tony C. T. Huang, Alexander Unterberger, Matthew Suderman, Carl Ernst, Michael J. Meaney, Gustavo Turecki, Moshe Szyf, Jörg Hoheisel. *Promoter-Wide*

Hypermethylation of the Ribosomal RNA Gene Promoter in the Suicide Brain. PLoS ONE, 2008; 3 (5): e2085 DOI: 10.1371/journal.pone.0002085

[30] Wei L, Hao J, Kaffman A (2014) *Early Life Stress Inhibits Expression of Ribosomal RNA in the Developing Hippocampus.* PLoS ONE 9(12): e115283.

[31] https://bigthink.com/philip-perry/the-bad-news-trauma-can-be-inherited-the-good-news-so-can-resilience

[32] Jovanovic T, etal. *Physiological markers of anxiety are increased in children of abused mothers.* J Child Psychology/ Psychiatry. 2011 Aug; 52(8):844-52. doi: 10.1111/j.1469-7610.2011.02410.x. Epub 2011 Apr 19

[33] The International SNP Map Working Group et al. *A Map of Human Genome Sequence Variation Containing 1.42 Million Single Nucleotide Polymorphisms* NATURE | VOL 409; 15 FEBRUARY 2001. www.nature.com.

[34] https://www.researchgate.net/figure/*Simplified-Master-NET-Chart-outlining-Meridians-Organs-Subluxation-sequences-Emotions*_fig2_23953124

Chapter Six:

[35] *The Innate Bases of Fear, From the Educational Department of the University of Birmingham* received for publication by Cyril Burt of the Editorial Board, April 29, 1929 291. Gibson, E. J., & Walk, R. D. (1960). *The "visual cliff."* Scientific American, 202, 67–71.

[36] Fantz, R. L. (1961). *The origin of form perception.* Scientific American, 204(5), 66–72.

[37] Kathleen M. Reilly. *What Kids Are Scared of—and Why: An age-by-age guide to what causes childhood fears and worries.* American Baby Magazine, May 2006.

Chapter Seven:
[38] Alex Grey. Excerpt from *Net of Being*

Chapter Eight:
[39] Dr. Joseph Brueur and Dr. Sigmund Frued. *Studien über Hysterie* by published 1895
Freud, Sigmund – Breuer, Joseph: *Studies in Hysteria. Translated by Nicola Luckhurst.* Penguin Books, London 2004.

Chapter Eleven:
[40] *Cerebral Metabolic changes in men after chiropractic spinal manipulation.* Alt Ther Health Med 2011 Nov-Dec; 17(6):12-7
[41] *On World Peace, Two Essays by the Holy Kabbalist Rav Yehuda Ashlag* © 2012 Kabbalah Centre International, Inc.

Chapter Fourteen:
[42] https://www.linkedin.com/pulse/mass-psychosis-our-time-marios-kyriazis
[43] https://rwmalonemd.substack.com/p/mass-formation-psychosis

Index

A

abuse	39, 67, 77, 106, 134
abuse, childhood	39
acupressure	99
acupuncturists	30, 97
adrenal glands	16
adrenaline	16
Adverse Childhood Experience (ACE)	39
agitation	76
aggression	19
allergy / allergies	77, 98, 101
Alpha waves	22, 23
Alpha-Theta waves	23
Alzheimer's disease	55
amygdala	19, 20, 21
amygdala hyper-responsivity	21
ancestors	64, 66
angels	xxv
anger	19, 20, 31, 54, 69, 106, 109, 119
anti-aging	106, 143
anti-stress effect	116
anxiety	xix, xxi, 8, 20, 22, 40, 78, 106, 108, 135, 150
apathy	20
applied kinesiology	41, 98, 115
ascending neural pathway	50
attachment theory	76
attention	36, 42, 76, 77, 84, 85, 99
attraction	xxii, 88
auric fields	8
auto-immunity	106
auto-immune disease	77
autonomic nervous system	17, 56, 57
axons	50

Index

B

back 68, 70, 78, 79, 85, 106, 108, 109, 137
back pain 46
behavior 8, 16, 31, 34, 41, 56, 57, 65, 69, 125
behavioral reactions 8
belief system 45
belonging 29
biochemical 45
biochemical process 65
bio-plasma 8, 30
blemish 119
blindness 91
blockages .... xvii, xviii, 42, 55, 115
blood 9, 16, 18, 42, 55, 66, 98, 100
blood analysis 98
blood pressure 18, 55, 98
body .... xvi, xvix, xxi, 3, 8, 10, 11, 18, 25, 30, 34, 35, 36, 42, 43, 44,
.... 47, 54, 97, 98, 106, 107, 115, 116, 118, 126, 134, 136, 143
bodymind 44
body-mind integration 71
body movement 106
bodily systems 116, 118
bones 100
boundaries 86
bowel movements 100 154
brain 7, 16, 17, 19, 20, 22, 23, 24, 33, 34, 44, 45, 55, 56, 57,
.... 58, 64, 65, 66, 77, 100, 107, 117, 149
breast 101
breath 42, 54, 100, 106, 107, 108
Broken Heart Syndrome 53, 54, 55, 56, 59, 149

C

cancer 9, 34, 55
cardiovascular disease 9
catatonic 4
cause 6, 7, 25, 49, 68, 69, 77, 78, 92, 115, 131, 133
cells .... xv, 55, 57, 64, 70, 98, 100
Central Meridians (see meridians) 30, 31, 36

chest pain ... 54
Chi (Qi) ... 30, 117
childhood ... 38, 39, 40, 41, 67, 75, 76, 106, 145, 148, 150
chiropractic adjustment ... 59
chiropractic spinal manipulation (CSM) ... 116, 117
chromosomes ... 70
chronic stress ... 9
circulation ... 18, 149
communication ... 20, 44, 56, 57, 66, 98, 99, 100, 115, 116, 149
Conception Vessel (see meridians) ... 31, 69
concussion ... 135
confidence ... 11, 78
conflict shock ... 34
connection ... ix, xviii, xxii, xxiii, 5, 16, 44, 49, 64, 70, 83, 87, 88, 120, 121
conscious ... 9, 34, 44, 45, 46, 77
consciousness ... xxiii, xxv, 35, 47, 48, 87, 99
convergent strabismus (cross eyes) ... 91
cortisol ... 16
cosmic effect ... 118
courage ... 35, 121
cranial brain ... 57
culture ... 77, 120

D

danger ... 10, 15, 40
death ... 6, 59, 65, 93, 149
deep grief ... 59
defense marker ... 107
defensive freezing ... 17
dehydration ... 100
denial ... 4
depression ... 20, 21, 40, 106
despair ... xxii, 35
developmental attachment ... 7
disease ... 5, 9, 30, 34, 44, 77, 92, 115
dissociative response (dissociation) ... 7
disintegration ... 4
disorganized attachment ... 7

Index

dissociation fragments 7
dissonance 98
Divinity 88
DNA sequence 67
dopamine 97
dread 30
dysfunction 97, 106, 143

E

ego 105, 119
electrical impulses 98
Electro-Encephalography (EEG) 22
electromagnetic 45
Emotion Regulation 20
emotional blockages xvii
emotional body 10, 11, 24
emotional distress 37, 47
emotional frequencies 31
emotional landmines 24, 33
emotional marker 77
emotional memory 107
emotional resonance response 35
emotional resonant frequencies 34
emotional rut 36
emotional shock 34
emotional splinters 19
emotional stress 9
emotional trauma 5, 8, 30, 31, 36, 42, 45, 48, 49, 54, 63, 68, 92,
.... 93, 108, 111, 115, 133, 135, 136, 145
energetic connection 88
energetic frequencies 20, 69
environment 78, 87, 120
epigenetic 63, 64, 65, 66, 70, 71
existence 4, 34, 109, 117, 119
expression 20, 32, 64, 71, 85, 99, 150

F

false pride 31-32
family ....ix, xii, xxi, 15, 17, 42, 46, 68, 91
fear ....xx, 4, 11, 19-22, 35, 39-40, 69, 75-78, 93, 118, 135
fear of falling 76
fear circuits 21
feelings 6, 8, 18, 30-31, 48-49, 69, 78, 117, 126
fight or flight 16, 67, 116
five love languages 84-86
freeze 16, 116
frequency 10, 22, 33-36, 45
friend 17, 86
frightened 9, 76
Functional MRI (fMRI) 20
functioning 7, 22, 98

G

ganglia 57-58
gastritis 134
gene activity (see epigenetics) 64
gene transcription 65
generation 32, 64, 67
genes 63-66, 70
genetics 63-64, 66-68, 70, 77
genome 64, 66-67
German New Medicine 34
German people 117
Germany 117
God ....xxiii, 32, 42, 87-88, 135
Governing Vessel (see meridians) 30-31
gratitude 79, 118
grief 20, 31, 35, 54, 59, 69, 86, 109
groggy 135

H

habits 44, 77, 92
harmony 98, 116-117
headache 4, 100, 106, 137

Index

health .... xv, 6, 9, 18, 39-41, 43, 45, 55, 70, 78, 83-84, 92, 99, ... 118, 143-144
heart .... xviii, xxiii-xxv, 18, 24-25, 34, 42, 48, 53-59, 69, 86-87, ... 108, 125, 145
heart attack 34, 54-55
heart-brain communication 57
heart chakra .... xxiv, 108
hippocampus 65
holding space 86
Holocaust .... ix, xx, 48, 66
hormones 16-18, 44, 54-55, 106
hugs 84-85
hydration / hydration reflex 98-100

I
illness .... xiii, 92
immune system 19, 116
impact .... xvii, xx, xxi, 43-44, 64-65, 69
index finger 99-100
inflammation 18, 64, 134
inheritance 63
iniquity 32, 67
instinct .... xxi, 19, 67, 76
intrinsic cardiac nervous system / ganglia 57-58
integrity 41, 98
interaction 56, 58, 88

J
joy 20, 41, 116-118, 120-121

K
kindness 87
kinesiology 41, 98, 115

L
life experiences 10, 64
Life-Force energy 20, 31, 36-37, 117-118, 120
light 87-88

liver 69
longevity 71, 105
loud noise 76
love .... ix, xxii, xxv, 36, 48, 83-88, 121

M
Magneto-Encephalograph manipulation 45
Malone, Robert MD 116-118
Map of Consciousness 35
Marios Kyriazis 115
Mass Formation Psychosis 115
mass hypnosis 116
medial prefrontal cortex (MPFC) memory 20-21
mercy 32-33, 67, 87
meridians 30-31, 36, 69
methylation 65-66
mind 6, 8, 18, 23, 29-30, 40-41, 43-45, 57, 70-71, 97, 106, 109, 115
mindfulness 24, 70-71
molecules 71, 97
MRI 20, 98
Munchausen Syndrome 77
muscle test 35, 41, 47, 68, 98-101, 107-109, 111 126

N
neck 11, 30, 42, 78-79, 106, 108-109, 116, 126, 135, 137
neglect 65, 85
neuro-cardiology 57
Neuro-Emotional Technique® (NET) 69
neurofeedback 68-69, 108
neurons 64-65
neurotransmitters 57, 97
nervous system 3, 7-8, 16-17, 19, 43, 56-58, 67, 76, 115-117
nurturance / nurture 31, 83-84, 86-88, 105, 126-127
nutrition 133-135

O
obesity 38-39
offspring 63-65

old age ... 37, 70
organ, dysregulation /deregulation ... xiii, 16, 20, 21, 58, 100, 134-135
origin ... 68, 93
overweight ... 39-40, 77-78
oxygen ... 59, 100

P
pain, emotional ... 45, 46, 47
pain, physical ... xiii, xiv, 78
pain, spiritual ... 78
paralysis ... 69, 91
parasympathetic nervous system ... 16, 56, 115
past, heal ... xviii
pathway ... 56, 57, 58, 98
peace ... 36, 109, 116
perception ... 16, 19
periaqueductal gray (PAG) region ... 16, 17
phenomena ... 92
physical abuse ... 39, 134
physical activity ... 59
physical body ... 10
physical gene characteristics and traits ... 63
physical symptom ... 107
physical therapy ... 117
physical touch ... 85
polarity ... 99
Positron Emission Tomography (PET) scanner ... 116
post-traumatic stress disorder (PTSD) ... xvii, xix, 7
presence ... 39, 70, 71, 85
pressure, blood ... 8, 55, 98
process ... 16, 20, 24, 36, 41, 43, 56, 63, 65, 79, 99, 105, 107, 108, 109, 116
psyche ... 119
psychological ... 44, 65, 66, 76
psychology ... 97

Q
Qi ... 30, 117

R

rage 20, 21, 30, 109
reactions 24, 33, 64
reality .... xx, 45, 69, 92
relationship .... xxi, xxii, xxv, 44, 77
research .... xiii, 7, 34, 43, 76

S

sadness 19, 31, 109
safety 15, 77,
security 8, 106
self-communication 98, 100
self-worth 17, 83, 118
sense 6, 7, 8, 16, 46
separation 46, 66
shame 30, 31, 35, 69, 119
shock .... xxiv, 4, 8, 34, 107
short-term 30, 58
Single Nucleotide Polymorphisms 67
situation 4, 8, 9, 16
sleep 22, 127, 135
solution/s 5, 6, 9, 39, 138
soul .... xxi-xxiii, xxv, 31, 87, 105
soul mate .... xxi-xxiii, 105
source .... xiv, 31, 92
spirit .... x, xxi-xxii, 30, 115
startle reflex 67, 107
storage warehouses of unfinished business 37
strain 15, 131
stress .... xvii, xix, 8, 9, 15-18, 44, 53
stress induced cardiomyopathy 53
stroke 34, 100
subconscious .... xx, 9, 20, 36, 44-6, 77
subjective emotional filter 9
suffering .... xxi, 5-6, 19, 32
suicide 64-5, 150
support 34, 42, 57, 127

Index

surface 25, 47, 111
survival 15, 21, 29, 48
sympathetic nervous system 16, 58, 67, 116
symptoms 4-5, 44, 54-5, 91-2, 135

T
Takotsubo Cardiomyopathy (Broken Heart Syndrome) 53-5, 149
telomerase enzymes 70
telomeres 70,
temporal lobe 21-2
tense 8, 11, 22, 29
tension 11, 15, 22
third eye 98-9
thought/s ....ix, 5, 21, 41, 55, 58
time ....xix-xxi, xxiii-xxv, 4, 7-9, 11, 15, 17-22, 32, 37
tissue 87
tools ....xxi, 86
trauma ....vii, xiii, xvii, xix-xxi, xxv, 3-8, 11, 17, 21-25, 30,37
traumatic brain injury (TBI) 22
traumatic environment 87
traumatic event 4, 24, 31-2, 36, 48, 98, 107
traumatic memory 43, 107-8
traumatized 7, 9, 19-20, 36, 48, 109
treatment 21, 46-7, 59, 68, 105, 116, 127, 135
trigger/s 20, 24, 33, 43, 68
trust ....xxiii, 35-6, 42-3, 106, 135

U
understanding 16, 44, 49, 55, 67, 86, 105
universal energy 87-88

V
ventromedial prefrontal cortex 20
victim 11, 29
vitality 38, 118, 121, 143-4
vulnerability 69

W
wall 17, 48-9, 87
water 41, 99, 100
world ....vii, x, xxiv, 11, 18, 33, 42, 56, 59

Y
Yin Tang Point 98, 99

Z
Zohar 119